Color Expressions

Color Expressions

AN ART EDUCATIONAL VOYAGE

Dr. Lonnie G. Ford

To order additional copies of this book, contact:
Xlibris Corporation
1-888-795-4274
www.Xlibris.com
Orders@Xlibris.com
67771

Contents

Chapter I

Chapter II

Chapter III

Chapter IV

Chapter V

I sincerely appreciate all the individuals whose cooperation, encouragement, and guidance made this study possible.

Preface

I am an art teacher. For the past 15 years, I have taught middle school students in an urban school district in metropolitan Detroit. My students learn how to draw, sketch, paint, and sculpt in a variety of media, ranging from pencils, to crayons, to water color, to clay, to fabric, to jewelry. They also learn important art concepts such as shape, pattern, texture, balance, symmetry, proximity, and closure. My students learn a lot about art in my class, and I enjoy teaching them. However, there is one thing about being an art teacher that has always frustrated me. Art does not receive the same respect as the other school subjects. Whenever budgets are tight, the art program is considered expendable. It is typically viewed by parents and educators as mere "enrichment" rather than a viable and essential part of the school curriculum.

Groups such as the National Art Education Association (NAEA) advocate for the importance of art by treating it as another core subject area that should be valued as highly as science, math, social studies, and language arts. While I generally agree with this stance, I think they are missing a critical argument for the value of art. By framing art as a stand-along core subject area, they neglect the essential connections among art and the other disciplines.

In this dissertation, I argue that art is not only important for its own sake, but is also a fundamental means through which students can learn the core subjects. As an art teacher, I teach more than "just" art. I also integrate math, science, social studies, and language arts into my art lesson plans in meaningful ways. Unlike any other art teachers whom I have encountered throughout my career, I actually align my lessons with the standards for the core subjects taken from the Michigan Curriculum Framework, and I also regularly communicate with my students' teachers in the core subjects in order to achieve curricular continuity in my classroom.

The purpose of this dissertation, which is framed as a qualitative autobiographical self-study, is to explore my own development as an art teacher and show how my unique approach to art education evolved from my personal experiences. Through telling my story, I hope to influence the decisions of policy makers regarding art education, in order to strengthen the position of art within the school community. I also hope to enlighten the practices of other art teachers who face the same kinds of frustrations and constraints that I have experienced.

Background of My Journey

Several years ago, I enrolled in a graduate course on educational research that focused on closing the achievement gap for African-American children. The course was structured to explore issues, causes and concerns for the achievement gap. Studying different educational outcomes, reading books and articles, we regularly shared our insights about some leading causes. Most importantly, we were instructed to stay within our subject areas when finding any contributions to that gap. In my attempt to complete the assignment of researching possible causes, in my discipline of art education, I found myself frustrated and angry. Why? There were no research studies exploring how art education was a part of the equation leading to solutions in closing the gap. In addition, there were no basic instructions or curricula designed to make connections to the art student to develop critical thinking skills or to incorporate the use of students' life experiences for learning. Furthermore, I felt that art education was used as a testing ground in urban schools, like the Chicago Public Schools using Teaching Artists to teach art with no teaching certification or teaching qualifications (Booth, 2003). The purpose of this approach was to use their knowledge and practices of art to influence change in students' learning. This kind of experiment branched away from any real effort to integrate art education and truly recognize it as a viable core subject area.

While conducting research for the course, I found that researchers defined the achievement gap between white and African-American students solely in terms of the four core subjects of math, science, social studies, and language arts, with no attention given to art education (e.g., Berlak, 2001, Honig, 2001, Limn, 2000, Sacks, 2000). A study by the National Black

Caucus entitled *Closing the Achievement Gap: Improving Education Outcomes for African American Children* (November, 2001) reports:

Make improving the literacy skills of students a top priority. Students who cannot read will experience little success in school. Reading is the key to academic achievement in every subject, ranging from math and English to science and history. We must put reading first by finding initiatives and programs designed to strengthen the reading skills of students, particularly low-performing students.

Again, there was no mention of art. As both an African-American and an art teacher, I found it very disturbing that the recommendations of many national and local art educational organizations and schools failed to address the importance of teaching art education in African-American urban school settings. My dissertation research ultimately arose from this concern.

Overview of the Contents

Chapter 1 focuses on my early childhood development in elementary school and how I used my environment as a tool for learning. My autobiographical narrative begins with a description of how I integrated art education concepts establishing a method for learning. Applying those self-taught methods and concepts, I became proficient in the four core subject areas and succeeded in school. The most significant obstacle that I encountered in my life, at this time, was the fact I lived in a high poverty area, also known as "The Projects". Most minorities are cut off from information, skills, and guidance that will prepare them for the pursuit of their desires to learn while living in a poverty area.

Moving from elementary to the junior high school, my learning environment changed. Following the *Brown v. Board of Education* decision desegregating public schools, I was bused to the neighboring school which was located in a predominantly white and more affluent neighborhood. This experience showed me the stark disparity between higher qualities of educational learning environment versus the destitution of living in a ghetto! While in junior high my educational art integration methods were slowed by national conflicts and catastrophic deaths of famous African-American people and the burning cities in the late 1960s'. These were my first encounters of how race relationships were so important to learning. In spite of the conflicts and tragedies around me, I was determined to remain focused on my education. I used art as a coping mechanism to deal with the events that surrounded me, and I came to understand the value of art as a way of learning.

During this time, I continually searched for the one teacher who would understand and endorse my use of art as a way of learning. The interesting thing about this search is that although I found several teachers like this in elementary and middle school, they were nowhere to be found in high school, college, and graduate school. I explain how this lack of guidance and understanding affected my academic success and achievements. With the school culture, social environment and unhappy classroom experiences, school became an illusion of unwanted relationships. For example, I was known more for my athletic abilities than for my unique artistic integrations in my learning, which I found extremely frustrating. While I enjoyed the attention that I received as an athlete, I longed for that one teacher or professor who would notice or appreciate the way I used art in my learning.

Chapter 2 focuses on the history of my employment as an art teacher and how I began to integrate art with the four core subject areas. All I needed was a place in which to put my theories into practice. My first opportunity came when I was hired to teach at a boys' home for underprivileged African-American adolescents who were wards of the state and were at risk of academic failure. My strategies were extremely successful. Later, as an art instructor for adult education, I continued to conduct more strategies to refine my teaching skills. I also describe in some detail, other positions that allowed me the opportunity to gain more knowledge in art education, use my strategies and attain my certification of teaching art education.

Chapter 3 consists of for my search for new ways to use art education for the purpose of teaching across the curriculum. This process began with my vision that all art teachers teach across the curriculum. I believe that a common set of standards, language and curriculum in art education can help teachers assess children's knowledge and skills. To accomplish this vision, it was imperative for me to attend workshops designed for teachers in the other core subject areas. While attending these workshops I would collect evidence that proved or disproved my strategies of the connections between art education and the core subject area. For example, attending a writing/reading workshop for language arts was particularly interesting and useful. The instructor had given us a writing assignment that caused a deep reflective regression to my childhood that had long been forgotten. This regression took me back to my heartbreaking childhood, making me revisit and review a time of despair. It was difficult for me to complete this writing assignment, but my instructors were so impressed my story that they got it published in a national writing journal.

Chapter 4 the review of the literature, that serves as a bridge between my personal story as an art educator and the broader field of art education.

It focuses on the failure of schools to adopt a common approach to Art Education, discusses the problems of Discipline-based Art Education (DBAE), the shortcomings of Teaching Artists, and misuses of technology. It is divided into three sections. In the first section, I present a detailed inventory of different national art educational organization's support of Fine Arts and not Art Education. In the second section, I describe the current practices in the classroom and how these national and local organizations give more financial support to those teachers who support and follow their methods of teaching art education. In the third section, I discuss the history and present use of technology in the art educational classrooms. Researching how technology is used in the classroom was extremely useful as a vehicle for elaborating my own beliefs, concepts, and practices today.

Chapter 5 includes an in-depth description of my current art pedagogy. I describe and evaluate three cross-curricular lessons that I have used with my students, providing vivid examples of how the core subjects can be taught in an art classroom. The first lesson was the defining of Art and Art Based Education so students can understand, comprehend, apply the strategies of art integration and learn the differences between them. The second lesson was about two point perspective and soft pastels. Students learn about the different views of perspective while constructing boxes, then coloring them with soft pastels. The third lesson was to create a Children's Storybook in a collaborative effort by students working in groups of three. Each student was assigned to one of three parts for completing the book which are the Artist, Author and Editor.

Currently, there is a lot of resistance through my research that I have found it difficult to believe that there is no substantial literature on the idea of integrating "art" into the content areas; no one talks about integrating the content areas into art classes.

Art educators tends to advocate for the status of art as a common area in it's own right with it own unique methods of knowledge and skills base that students should learn from art teachers. Furthermore, there is a lot of resistance to my idea among art teachers, who feel that integrating the content areas into art class will detract from the teaching of art. I'm suggesting since there is nothing out there, that my research may prove to be quite original.

Since I am the object of this study, it is a humbling feeling and an honor to share my story through personal narratives from childhood to adulthood. I hope to bring a clear perspective on an art education proposal that draws the national organizations and local art educators together. My vision is to create a common language for art education and improve the ways in which art is experienced by urban school students.

Acknowledgements

I sincerely appreciate all the individuals whose cooperation, encouragement, and guidance made this study possible.

I am grateful to my academic advisors and professor, and to the members of my doctoral committee Dr. James Muchmore, Dr. Sue Poppink and Dr. Ronald Crowell. Their insight and knowledge have provided many helpful suggestions that have contributed to the completion of my research and professional growth and development'

+I also wish to express gratitude to my former professors at Western Michigan University, Kalamazoo. Their instructions and course work prepared me for this study. Special thanks go to Dr. Ann Kopy for editing sections of my dissertation. I would like to thank my family for their patience throughout this study, and for bringing so much happiness into my life.

Finally, I dedicate this study to my father, David William Ford Sr. and my mother, Lois Juanita Ford, both have passed, who's dream of my achieving my educational goal, receiving my doctoral degree, has manifested. I know both of them are proud of me, I only wish they were here in the flesh not the spirit, so they could share this awesome and incredible accomplishment.

Lonnie G. Ford

Chapter I

MY EARLY YEARS

My story begins at my home in the Projects in the Township of Royal Oak, Michigan. Living with my mother, three sisters and brothers, at times with my father, I was next to the baby in the family. The Projects were divided into two different school districts, one Oak Park School, the other Ferndale. We were part of the Oak Park School District, but we had a Ferndale address, post office and zip code. The Projects were manufactured homes, funded by the government, from army barracks used by soldiers from a nearby army base. The barracks were abandoned by the army at the end of War World II. At that time, the industrial revolution was occurring and there was a mass exodus from the South to the North. Because there was a severe housing shortage, the barracks were torn down and replaced with two-story townhouses. These manufactured homes were like townhouses of today, just built with poor quality materials like paper thin walls so you could hear every argument by the neighbors, pressed wood for the homes, porches and fences and left over paints etc.

Like townhouses, the homes were connected in units, with each unit consisting of six homes with small front and backyards. You were one of the fortunate families if you lived on the end of the unit, because the front and backyards were connected, which made your house appear to be bigger! Those yards that were connected were fenced in with white wooden posts, white gates, with gray crossed linked metal fencing secured by large gray metal nails with flat heads. One thing that was so impressive about these homes were the colors they used – greens, blues and yellows to paint the homes. Most of the homes were painted greenish yellow, bluish-green trimming along the roofline and window frames, with light bluish sea foam green front doors. The backdoors were painted a dark jungle green, the same color as the roof. I realized that even at a young age color and an artistic perspective impacted my world, which will be further discussed in chapter two.

The streets were paved with charcoal black asphalt with just enough room for two cars to pass each other, side-by-side. The streets flowed through the units that resembled the shape of two wide six tooth gapped hair combs laid down on the ground side-by-side, with the teeth of the combs being the streets. The homes were facing across each other in standard two-by-two formations. Connecting these two combs, in the center, was one main street that connected the teeth (streets) with one way in and one way out, which was at the top of the two combs. The other units were designed in the same manner, which led to a "main drag" (one street that connected the streets from the unit that provided a way out to where other streets led to different towns or highways).

A single light grayish looking sidewalk, which was connected from those streets, led to wooden steps and porches located in front of the houses. There were no driveways, so cars had to park on the right side of the street, which at times caused some frustration to the people who were trying to get past but could not. Those who were frustrated had to go door to door in search of the owners of the vehicles that were impeding their progress. Once the owner was found, asking them to move their vehicles proved taxing, because harsh words were exchanged, the kinds of words a young man should not be exposed to. After saying the last few words, the owners eventually moved their vehicles to allow passage.

Bone Chilling Winter

During the winter, the snowplows could not get by, so they would plow the snow along side and in front of the parked vehicles. The snowplow piled this grayish white snow so deep that it usually covered the entire parked car. The owners had a very difficult time trying to shoveling their way out because it was a mixture of black asphalt and snow. It was like getting out of a giant cocoon. They shoveled for hours! If seeing your vehicle in a cocoon wasn't enough reason to remove it, the worst was yet to come! This huge fire engine red dump truck, with big jet-black wheels and the two black faced white men who drove it, delivering brick sized coal that was used for our coal burning furnaces. The men stopped, dumped the jet-black coal on the white snow covering the streets, in front of homes on one side of the street then the next day the other side. If there were vehicles blocking the streets, they would go to the next street. My brothers and I had to pick the coal up with shovels, put it into a large silver pale with a sturdy handle, and transport it from the streets onto the front porch into the coal bin. This partially explained how I develop my strength at an early age. I was kind of chubby, but I had very strong muscles and talent hidden from view, but it was freezing to the bone!

Summer Haze

During one of those hot muggy bright sunny days of summer, the sunshine caused a phenomenon that was fascinating and something occurred that I would never forget! The sun had heated the dark streets, like a grill heating up black charcoal, causing thick wavy lines to dance toward the sky. The sunshine reflected off the windows into the wavy pattern creating a cosmic fingerprint of colors as you looked down the street. I tried sharing this treasure with others in my family and they told me they couldn't see it! Only my second eldest sister said she observed and experienced my visual images, but I know she didn't; she was the one who always sheltered me and protected from harm.

> The years of early childhood are the time to prepare the soil. Once the emotions have been aroused-a sense of the beautiful, the excitement of new and the unknown, a feeling of sympathy, pity, admiration or love—then we wish for knowledge about the object of our emotional response". "Once found, it has lasting meaning". "It is more important to pave the way for the child to want to know than to put him on a diet of facts he is not ready to assimilate. (Carson, 1956, p. 45).

Grand Façade

It was apparent that the designed environment and layout of my home was an integral part of my artistic birth. My home was my childhood environment for learning and discovering during my early years. Environment education based on life experiences should begin during the very earliest years of life. Such experiences play a critical role in shaping life-long attitudes, values, and patterns of behavior toward natural environments (Tilbury, 1994). Every room was like an artist's smorgasbord of visual delight. These descriptors are used to explain the development of my artist journey and my current ideology for teaching

Art Education. These experiences are the effects that, through my eyes, drive the very heart and soul of my dissertation.

As you approached the front of our house there was a white wooden gate to welcome you. Opening the gate, a short grayish white cement sidewalk would lead you to four bluish light green wooden steps that you use to walk up onto the porches in front of the house. To the left, a large bluish white rectangular wooden pole supporting a dark forest green overhanging roof that covered the entire porch. To the right, about three feet from the floor of the porch, a wooden picture framed the door with a latch and key lock. This was used to store coal for our coal-burning furnace. Two steps ahead a large bluish green light door had a screen door, which was nothing more than a large rectangle shaped wooden frame with a gray metal screen fastened to it with smaller gray flat headed nails bent to one side. Attached to the side connected to the wall by two hinges was a long, tube-shaped, gray spring connecting to the inside center of door. Opening the front door, you stepped directly into the kitchen, with a black and white checkerboard tiled floor with a light salmon pink with jet-black trimming colored molding. To the left, a huge white marble looking table with silver metal trimming and legs stood proud knowing it could seat our entire family for Sunday's special dinners. I spent a lot of time at this table drawing, coloring and doing my homework. On the other side of table next to the wall was a huge eggshell white refrigerator with silver handles. To the right was a door that led to the coal burning furnace, then a wall with a light white sink and stove.

Walking straight ahead into the next room was the living room with eggshell white walls, dark jungle-green trim and molding and dark shiny sepia brown hardwood floor. My mother would spend hours washing and waxing that floor making it clean enough to eat off! To the left stood my father's big soft padded light beige high back chair with pine green swirling flowers. The fabric was secured by small golden pins along the back edges, in front of the armrests in circular pattern, down to the base surrounding the chair, with four short square-shaped dark cherry legs. Those golden pins in the chair resemble metal rivets holding steel columns together in buildings. The seat cushion was a big fluffy pillow, soft yet firm. My father, after a hard day at the auto factory, would come home, sit in that chair and fall asleep! A large turquoise-blue hourglass shaped lamp, with a large beige lampshade, was sitting on a dark wooden cherry end table that stood next to the chair. All four legs resembled long question marks with a shelf connecting them, which was used for magazines and other books. Against the wall, a soft padded dark olive green armchair with a comfortable pillow seat faced the coach across the room. This seat cushion was a big pillow sewn with thread instead of metal pins as was the entire chair. Next to the chair a dark mahogany rectangular cabinet containing a part record player, radio, and television, stood with short legs angled toward the corner of the room. The television could be viewed from every point of the living room, except from the armchair, unless you were very tall or had a long neck that stretched like E.T.!

On that same wall, a large light lime-green picture window, seeming as though it had been cut out of the wall, was framed by white shear curtains. The curtains were wrapped around a thin white metal pole at the top of the window frame, which sat on white metal units that looked like two cup-shaped hands, attached to the end of the frame mounted on the wall. The curtains, draping to the floor, had curling mint-green stems with maroon-red poppy flowers with a light dandelion-yellow bud center at the end of each curling stem, which captured light and unleashed rays of life into the living room. Also, my mother kept her two large potted forest—green plants there. One pot was light apricot-pink and the other shell-white with matching plates on the bottom. During Christmas, we pulled the curtains apart displaying our brightly lit multicolored Christmas trees.

To the right, a large low back dark olive-green three-seat cushion, matching the armchair, sat against the wall. The three cushions were like big soft pillows, which at times when I was ill, my mother had me lay down on to comfort me. These couch cushions were much softer than the bed that I slept on. Talk about rest! When I slept on those cushions, it was always the best sleep ever! The floor of the living room was a shiny dark sepia-brown hardwood covered with a large room size light spring green area rug. On top of the rug there was a light cream-colored coffee table that was as long as the couch and almost as wide as the rug. On top of the coffee table, a cut piece of clear glass fit evenly, so as to protect the table from spills or things being placed there and kept it always clean and sparkling. At the back of the living room, to the right, there was a dark jungle-green metal door with a silver doorknob and matching hinges. It had a keypad lock with no windows and was always kept closed. We seldom used this door because it had no screen door on the outside and when opened lots of dirt would find its way inside, which was unacceptable to my mother.

The upstairs had the most effect on me; it became my refuse, my paradise island, my hidden tower of solitude. As you stood, with your back against the back door, you faced the stairway with twelve dark burnt sienna-brown wooden steps that led you upstairs to a small hallway. The dark burnt sienna hallway connected the bathroom and the bedrooms. The dark forest-green walls continue from the bottom to the top of the stairway. The only light source visible was a single huge uncovered light bulb, attached by short thick jet-black wire, which hung from the ceiling. The light was controlled by two light switches, one on the right side of the wall at the bottom of the stairway. The other switch was on the left side of the wall just outside of the bathroom door. Next to the bathroom was the door to my parents' room. My parent's room was off limits! We were told never to use their room as a playroom, but occasionally I would sneak in without their knowledge. There was this enormous bed that took up most of the room! It had a wooden raw sienna headboard, a light mint green bedspread with little tassels hanging all around the edges. Those same dark colored hardwood floors, similar to the floor in the living room, covered the room. Next to the bed was a soft, small, lime green square colored rug on the entrance side of the bed. Crawling under the bed, I would imagine myself in the thick green-jungle of Africa waiting quiet and patiently to shoot any animal that came in view.

Next to my parents' room, in the hallway, there was a shelving unit that stored all of our lining, extra pillows, blankets, cleaning products, a big burnt orange colored picnic basket that was used as a sewing kit and other things needed for the upstairs. My mother provided me with this awesome piece of furniture, an old fashioned wooden indian-red school desk, which sat in front of that shelving unit. This became my fortress of solitude. The desktop was large enough to hold all of my crayons, drawing paper and pencils. There was this deep carved out groove near the top of the desktop's edge. That groove was deep enough to stop my pencil from rolling off the top, because the desktop tilted down slightly and inward toward a chair. This dark-gray heavy metal frame connected the desktop to a chair on the right side, which prevented you from completely siding across the seat. Underneath the chair was an opening that I had used to store my books, extra paper and pencils. The chair had small heavy thick gray metal legs, so my mother placed an old thin olive-green rug under the desk to avoid scratching her beautiful shiny hardwood floor. This chair became a portal to embark into a different dimension. While sitting in the chair, I felt as though I were the commander at the helm of a spaceship. The desktop became the control panel (the con) where the navigation toggle buttons and switches were found. Pushing a certain button on the con a star chart would appear with illuminating bluish white holographic images of planets and constellations. Selecting a destination from the star chart, a course was plotted and punched into the directional system. The switches and buttons on the con glowed with interrupted flashes of fluorescent green, red and yellow lights on my face. As the engines engaged, my feet began feeling a slight tingling vibrating sensation, like the tuning fork the doctor places on your knee. That sensation slowly spiraled up my legs through my body. This reaction occurs when the engine's thrusters explode to its maximum output, the result is light speed!

Reaching my destination, a grayish planetoid beyond the last moon of Pluto, the navigational system placed me into a perfect orbit. Orbiting this planetoid, I discovered that the land and seascapes were that same grayish color as its atmosphere. Maneuvering the ship slowly into the atmosphere, under manual control, a decision on how to breathe the color of life into this planetoid was made. Flying through the atmosphere, silver canisters with powerful detonators were prepared and deployed at strategic positions around the planetoid. These silver canisters look like giant paint cans without handles. Their contents are this thick super gloss multicolored liquid paint that when released ignites into multi-colored flames on contact. One by one the canisters fell towards its targets. Before contact with the ground the sensors sent an electronic impulse that detonated the canisters. The canisters exploded like underwater depth chargers dropped by a U-Boat. Several colorful mushroom clouds formed releasing millions of tiny, sparkling, thick, milky droplets of liquid that danced across the sky. The dancing droplets looked like sparks from an arch welder's torch as it mixed with the atmosphere. A spectacular dazzling display of electric colors of joy dripped everywhere and on everything! Making the sounds of thousands of T-Bone steaks on a hot grill, the droplets quickly consumed the area. The land moved like water as the metamorphosis of the planetoid began. The most impressive phenomenon occurred as the ocean's water became this shimmering, clear, light, emerald yellowish blue, like the lights that reflect off the spinning glass Disco Ball from above the dance floor. Returning to my original orbit, this once grayish planetoid was now this big glowing light green marble, with white billowing clouds swirling, embracing and rotating around its new skin! Nevertheless, with each adventure I found myself in a daze of timeless motion admiring my handy work. Each time a strong bright greenish blue magnetic light would surround my ship and take over the con. The powerful light would pull me towards home base leaving only the communication system in tact with an urgent voice message, "Wash your hands, it's time to eat"!

The door to my sister's bedroom was next, as you turn to the right and the door of my bedroom faced you. As you walk into my bedroom, the light switch was on the left wall with a yellow switch plate and the walls were painted greenish-blue. There were three beds with their headboards against the far wall. One was an army bunk bed and the other was a regular twin size bed. The bunk bed had a dark wood grain metal head and footboards, with two small metal large bolts with a flat head turned sideways, located underneath and inside on each leg. A dark-gray metal mattress frame was attached to the head and footboards by two small c-shaped hooks at both ends and on the sides that could be easy to hook on and secure. The frame had small gray metal springs that crisscrossed from side to side and top to bottom, connecting as they crossed to form large rectangles. It supported a gray cloth covered all wooden box frames and a twin size gray and white striped mattress. These mattresses were standard for soldiers issued in the army barracks. These mattresses were so thin they could easily be rolled up into a large striped ball. My bedroom had a hardwood floor which was a light burnt sienna and had a large pictured framed window at the other end of the room. I shared this room with my three anxious brothers. Now, my three brothers didn't support or encourage my efforts for isolation and expressed concerns of my failure to enthusiastically seek friendships or play with the other children in the neighborhood. They would take pictures I had drawn off the bedroom walls and destroy them. This was their cruel way in a feeble attempt to try to get me to abandon my thoughts of seclusion in the bedroom and eventually leave the house. My brother liked to kick the box frame from underneath mine, which raised the mattress, at night too! He continued trying to scare me by telling me, "It's an earthquake"! Their attempts were unsuccessful and proved to be an enormous task they could not achieve, so they left me alone. My eldest brother slept in a bed alone, across the room closest to the window. He was lucky, too! For instance, during some of those hot muggy summers nights, the wind billowed cool air into the room through the window. Those cool breezes found him first and never seemed to get to the rest of us. The curtains didn't help at all! They were long, heavy, dark turquoise-green, and cloth-like, and touched the floor. The side facing the window was this white quilt-like texture, with tiny grooves, that kept the cold air out during the freezing winters. So, when a nice cool refreshing wind blew in from the window, especially during those hot sweltering summer nights, it blocked the air from relieving the sauna-like condition of my side of the room.

Next to the window, the wall extended into the area that we used like a walk in closet without doors. There was a built-in wooden shelf the length of the closet with a white-apricot pole attached underneath. Hanging on the pole with golden metal hangers were all my worldly clothing possessions; six shirts and three pair of pants. Not having enough clothing aided my decision to stay inside. If I went out to play, the other children would tease and humiliate me for wearing the same clothing every day. I owned six shirts. One was a longed sleeved white dress shirt that I wore only to church; the second was multicolored with stripes, red white and blue, with tiny flowers and a patch pattern on both the elbows. The third was a pullover that was an olive-green velvet-like material with a brown square string in front, instead of buttons. This string started at the chest and ended at the neckline. Of the three pairs of pants, I had dress black slacks, which I used for church, faded blue jeans and dark jungle-green corduroy, which were called "my school clothes". On the closet floor two pairs of shoes sat quietly. One pair was jet-black slip on dress shoes, and the other was a newer pair of black and white Red Ball Jets gym shoes. The black shoes were worn to church, the other pair to school.

Let me tell you about Red Ball Jets; they were the hottest and latest style for gym shoes, like the Air Jordan's Nike swoop of today! Their symbol, a little red ball on the back knee of the shoe could make you bounce higher and run faster!

Standing there, staring into the closet at my wardrobe, a veil of make believe was lifted from my face. My mind and body began swirling, just like that enormous dark gray tornado, the one that threw Dorothy out of Kansas into the Land of Oz, where she landed with a thud! Her head still spinning, she walked to the front door, opened it slowly and all at once bright vibrant colors leaped into the house soaking Dorothy with the wellspring of life. Only for me, the door began closing, the watercolors of life and light that drenched the room ran out of the house like a thief in the night, taking the energy of life and light away. Everything was my imagination, a dream . . . . not reality. For instance, those white wooden fences that surrounded the homes were just some resemblance of white. They were this ashy washed out grayish color and the metal fences were rusted and half buried in the ground. The street had large potholes, littered with broken pop bottle glass and paper trash. On the playgrounds, the play equipment had at least one broken swing to every swing set, lots of tall grass that covered abandoned cars and other items thrown away as trash. Others might view my world, this place that I lived, a "ghetto", because I was . . . . poor.

Drawing, Coloring and Schooling

Trying to organize and get a sense of being I tried co-existing in the "real world" by integrating art into my learning arena. In elementary school my teachers grew very impatient with me. During math I would be drawing pictures, and then coloring them instead of working out the math problem on paper. Creating these wonderful pie charts using different colors with bright yellows, blues and greens was my tool for learning. When my crayons and pencil were taken away, this was torturous punishment. Not being allowed to draw or color shut down all my desires to learn. Drawing and coloring made learning relevant to me! This one teacher would say, "Your drawing and coloring has nothing to do with your math,

science, reading or the world events". I knew she was wrong because I
learned my multiplication tables by drawing pictures and coloring the
answers different colors.

For example, in 2 x 2 = 4, I would color the number four green; next
in 2 x 3 = 6, I would color the number six blue and so on up to the ninth
place. Since the box of crayons had eight colors, the zeros, ones and
tens were not colored. Remembering how to multiply by zero, ones and
tens was easy. First, I would draw a large tree with leaves making the tree
branches the problem, and then put the answers on the leaves. So, even
if the teacher wrote any multiplication problems on the board, in any
order, following my color scheme ensured that, if called on, my answers
would certainly be correct! It was so amazing that nobody knew of my
secret, that creating my own world of learning and watching it come to
life was not a fantasy! Ginsberg & Wlodkowski (2000) wrote:

> We all ought to consider artistry as an embedding of art in
> learning rather than as a separate and frequently disenfranchised
> experience. Knowledge is barren without the capacity for feeling
> and imagination. Art is a fundamental part of life and learning
> across cultures. We believe the lack of meaning that is often
> attributed to academic learning is due to a significant extent
> to the separation of learning from imagination and artistry.
> Imagination and artistry can be used in every subject area. Both
> processes are open ended and serve as kindling for creative
> possibilities and academic goals (p. 158-9).

Somehow my artistic ability spread throughout the school. Maybe it
had something to do with the way I gave my drawings to other students so
they would like me and take them to their classrooms to share them with
other students and teachers. I'm sure the teachers asked who the artist was
because many teachers came to my classroom asking for me. They wanted
me to create, draw and color background scenery for puppet shows and
plays for their classroom. I loved all the joyous occasions of the holiday;
seasons were the best of times. The school was decorated with several of
my creations for the season, but when it came to my own personal works
of art, it seems as though everyone's mind closed. They were confused and
could not understand my explanation of bright colors of patterns across
the paper. The teachers had no clue what to say to me or how to grasp
the interpretation of my artwork, yet they were still supportive enough
to encourage my growth as an artist. "If a child is to keep alive his inborn
sense of wonder . . . he needs the companionship of at least one adult who
can share it, rediscovering with him the joy, excitement, and mystery of

the world we live in" (Carson, 1956, p. 45). However, one teacher told me "to keep my day job," a phrase which I came to understand with greater clarity as an adult. She was telling me I wasn't good enough to make it.

During that time in America, busing was the government's way of achieving racial integration in schools. Our school district served a predominately Jewish community, (about 97%), with about 2% African-Americans, and 1% Arab-Americans. The cities of Oak Park and Royal Oak Township are located just northwest of the city of Detroit, and the elementary school I attended was one and a half miles from the middle school. In our school district busing was not an issue. We had no choice but to ride the buses to attend one of two middle schools or the one high school. To get to middle school, I rode this big huge bright shiny canary-yellow bus, with coal-black trim tires interior and dark pine-green seats. Riding on the bus exposed my eyes to a neighborhood that had no abandoned cars on streets covered by tall thick jungle-green weeds; the streets had no holes or trash and even the birds were different colors. The ramification of this experience was like watching a black and white movie that was suddenly colorized. As we turned into what appeared to be a street, I was amazed to discover that this was actually the driveway leading to the front of the school.

The school was a brand new beautiful light-gray brick building with light blue trimming around the windows that gleamed in the sunlight and a long roof that extended from the front doors along the driveway. As we approached the school, the driveway circled around a parking lot full with brand new polished cars, in different sizes, colors and shapes, until it stopped in front of the school where the roof extended. There were two other buses that stopped where the blue metal poles supported the flat extended roof. This extended roof was a convenience; it protected us from the elements while exiting the buses. Walking under the flat roof towards the entrance, there were six freshly painted dark sky-blue doors, with one rectangular shaped window on each door. The window measured about six inches in width by twenty-four inches in length that started just above the silver door handle, up the right side of the door two inches from the doorframe. Opening the door and entering the building, bright colors of indigo-blues and yellow harvest-gold hit me, like the rushing wind of a warm hurricane, from a shiny light sandstone floor that was blinding. The light came from large silver framed picture windows, the likes I never seen before. Standing there blinking, rubbing my eyes and wishing this was not a dream, the urge came over me that this door wouldn't close! As I had dreamt before using my childhood imagination, my feelings resembled those of Dorothy when she opened the door to discover she was in Oz. Walking down the hallway, there were signs displaying that the school colors were blue and gold and the nickname of the school was the Falcons. With a big grin, like the *Grinch Who Stole Christmas*, I knew that I was no longer in Kansas!

Now, being with a different ethnic group did not change my approach to learning in school. My art skills expanded along with integrating those skills into the different subject areas, which prepared me for tests, quizzes, solving problems and homework. Most of my teachers were not interested in my method of learning until my seventh grade science class. This teacher was phenomenal! After talking with him about my artistic abilities, he encouraged the use of my artistic skills to draw the lab experiments for notes and homework. He even let me draw Spiderman in class! Due to this fact, after exposing Spiderman's true identity as a science student, the teacher got my attention. With much feeling and admiration, my description of how Spiderman created his webbing by mixing different formulas together put a smile on that teacher's face. All of my dreams had finally come true. It was good kismet to find someone who embraced my thoughts, skills and knowledge, and let me use my talents for learning.

Science was one of my favorite subjects, because other science teachers, also, encouraged me to continue using my artistic skills in their classrooms. Although they would not let me draw Spiderman in class, they did encourage my artistic skills for lab experiments and notes. My other teachers didn't support the use of my art in my learning; most of them told me that you must learn to write good notes if you ever want to get into college.

It is reasonable to say that I was in search of a learning framework Gardner (2005) discusses three characteristics for searching for such a framework: the intuitive, the traditional student and the discipline expert. First, the intuitive learner (known hereafter as the natural, naïve or universal learner), is the young child who is superbly equipped to learn language and other symbolic systems and who evolves serviceable theories of the physical world and of the world of other people during the opening years of life. Second, the traditional learner (or scholastic learner), which spans roughly from age seven to twenty, is one who seeks to master the literacy, concepts and discipline forms of the school. Third, the discipline expert (or skilled person), is an individual of any age who has mastered the concepts and skills of a discipline or domain and can apply such knowledge appropriately in new situations.

Of these three characteristics, my learning style tended to resemble the intuitive learner. Gardner (2005) also stated that the intuitive learner reflects neurobiological and developmental constraints — constraints owing to species membership and principles of human development that operate predictably in physical and social environments encountered all around the world.

The development of my note taking came after studying Leonardo da Vinci. He developed his own way of writing notes in his drawing journal (he wrote from left to right instead of right to left) and that influenced my creative mind to flow. Using the standard sized ruled paper, there was enough room to place two sentences within the spaces of the lines. This saved lots of paper and discouraged others from borrowing my notes because they could not read them. When the teachers checked my notes, they complained that my notes were too small and impossible to read. My response to them was always the same—that reading my notes was not a problem for me. "Besides," I would say, "You told me to learn how to take notes." So, in learning how to take notes, writing small, saving on paper, and aggravating teachers became my modus operandi!

At this time around the country, there was civil unrest in many cites across this nation, especially those cities with large minority populations. The assassination of Dr. Martin Luther King, shouts of racism, equality, bigotry and riots scared this nation, threatening to tear it apart. Cities were burning, African American people looting, some being shot at by police; and some were being killed, business properties were destroyed if they did not display the slogan "Soul Brother" on the building. That same army base, near my home, deployed trucks loaded with white men dressed in full jungle-green battle gear armed with M-16 rifles. The soldiers were assigned the task of protecting the firemen who were trying to extinguish burning buildings in the ghettos of Detroit. There were a lot of very angry citizens who disapproved of the efforts of the firemen trying to control the burning of those buildings. The burning of buildings became a rallying symbol in protesting the social injustices felt around the country by African-Americans. The tension of the riots from Detroit reached the city of Oak Park on Friday, May 1, 1970 at the high school; there was fighting among black and white student! While I was in my English class, an announcement came over the middle school's intercom system asking that all the African-American students had to report to the cafeteria immediately! Once in the cafeteria, the principal provided us with information regarding the situation at the high school. This surprised me because at the middle school the race relationship I thought was great and we all were very respectful toward each other. We were given the choice of leaving or staying in school and told that the buses were waiting outside to transport those students who wanted to leave. Only two of us decided to stay. My decision was for educational reasons and nothing else, but for the other female student who stayed I never knew her reason, even to this day. I have seen her on several occasions as an adult and we have never talked about it. While boarding the buses, many of the African-American students called me names like "Uncle Tom", "Whitey lover" and "stupid"! Then while walking back to my class, a white Jewish boy decided to interrogate me about other African-American male behavior toward him as he left the building. Several girls stood up in my defense and told him to leave me alone. On Monday, the high school re-opened with the presence of law enforcement officers in the building and all of the African-American students who left the middle school returned. Soon things returned to normal, at least on the surface.

Another significant event that changed my life personally was when my family moved from The Projects into a newly constructed, single dwelling, four bedroom brick-red house, with a gray flat roof, a long large driveway and a large front and fenced backyard with jungle green grass. For the first time in my life, I had a room to myself. My mother purchased all new furniture; she didn't want to relocate any of those small uninvited guests (cockroaches). These events, the assassination of Martin Luther King, Jr., the Vietnam War, the looting and burnings of large cities, and race riots around the country and at my high school, shook the very foundations of the depth of my soul, etching memories that will live on for all the days of my life.

As the nation cooled off, my high school days began with some surprises. That huge canary yellow bus looked smaller as it pulled up to the bus stop. My head now touched the ceiling, forcing me to walk like the hunchback of Notre Dame as I moved down the now skinny aisle. It was strange and finding a seat proved difficult as well. Not only could my body not fit, but my legs had to extend into the aisle to sit comfortably. If that was not enough, the bitter feelings of anger and resentment remained from the incident regarding my decision to stay at school during the riot. Those dagger-like looks being thrown directly towards the target were heart felt. Eventually, riding the bus created a situation that proved too much for me, just unbearable. Every day I was being challenged and threatened with bodily harm by African-American boys. Fighting was not an option because I was vastly outnumbered. I walked home that day and found other means of transportation back and forth from high school.

The high school was a sand dune colored brick building. Being the last person off the bus, I stood there imagining how I had thought the middle school was huge, but the high school was three times bigger; it was enormous. It too, had a flat roof extension to a circle driveway supported by snapdragon red metal poles. The four metal entrance doors were painted the same color as the poles. Upon entering into the school, the floor tiles were this bright tumbleweed light brown that reflected the colors of carmine red and feather white. These were our school colors and our nickname was the "Redskins". Immediately, I instituted a search for teachers who might appreciate and support my methodology for learning, which proved fruitless. Not one teacher understood the skills and techniques and enthusiasm for integrating my drawing abilities into their subject area. Discovering that my artistic abilities were not appreciated, not in the least, was like tasting bitter herbs and I had to swallow the pill of academics. Any artistic innovations or ideas that I showed to the teachers were constantly brushed aside.

The Jock

Most of the teachers came to know me only as a "jock", as my athletic contributions overshadowed my artistic skills. They even made up a nickname for me! I was known as "The Big Red Machine". Playing football, basketball and then track and field impressed more teachers, the student body, and even several college coaches. My athleticism impressed enough coaches for me to receive offers of full athletic scholarships from several major universities. As for my pursuits of finding that one teacher who connected with me, I had no luck and I felt like just another student. For the rest of my high school days, the excitement of learning diminished. Gardner (2005) states that knowledge is developed in a young person in two different routes, "mimetic" education and the "transformative" approach. With "mimetic" education, the teacher demonstrates the desired performance or behavior and the student duplicates it as faithfully as possible. The "transformative" approach, rather than modeling the desired behavior, the teacher serves as a coach or facilitator, trying to evoke certain qualities or understandings in the students. Definitely, my learning style displayed a transformational approach and finding that teacher that would encourage my learning process, proved to be a daunting task in itself. Gardner (2005) also writes that adherents of the basic-skills approach stress the need to master certain literacy's and skills, such as the venerable three R's and body of factual knowledge of, say, history, geography, and science. Any additional learning must be created upon the solid basic; basic-skills proponents have often insisted, "One must crawl before one can walk". Finally, Gardner writes "that ultimately any form of learning requires performance, be it a copy of the master's rendition of a song or a transformation of that rendition in an original form; production of a rote or a reconfigured network of the data; recitation of a fixed body of scientific principles or a use of such principles to solve-or even define-a new problem" (p. 119-120). All that was left from my innovations and ideas was my note taking, which has stayed with me even today.

What made matters worse, all of the art classes were offered as electives. This was insulting and cruel because I form the notion that art should be part of the core curriculum, not an elective. Fortunately, my eagerness to sign a full athletic scholarship to play football at a major college renewed a spirit that had lain dormant.

College Bound

The college that earned the rights to my body was located miles away from my home. This would be the first time I had ever been separated from my family and my comfortable surroundings. Arriving on the campus of Central Michigan University, colors of maroon and dark daffodil yellow-gold waved from the several flags, signpost, names of buildings and banners welcoming incoming freshman and visitors. The nickname of the college, "Chippewas", which was in the center of most of the signs and banners, was printed in that dark daffodil yellow-gold or a giant "C" on other displays.

Checking into my dorm room, the level of expectations changed because my every waking moment was now dominated by football practice. My day began with football practice from 6:00 to 8:00 in the morning in order to beat the heat of the day. The stadium had a soft dark green leaf colored artificial turf painted with snow white lines that bordered the field and yard lines crossing the field. When artificial turf heats up, it is always ten degrees hotter than the temperature reported nearby. I had never seen or ever walked on artificial turf before, so stepping on this turf sounded like and felt like crushing thousands of tiny hay straws standing up on ends, only to spring back up once you lifted your foot.

After practice, breakfast was served from 9:00 am until 10:00 am at the dorm. So, I had to move expeditiously to the shower, dry off and get dressed quickly. From 11:00 am until 2:00 pm, was usually down time and most of the players slept or just laid in bed trying to recover from the soreness of hitting blocking pads, tackling dummies, blocking sleds and each other. From 12:00 pm until 1:00 pm, lunch was served. Subsequently, practice began again at 3:00 pm and lasted until 5:00 pm. Afterwards, dinner was served at 6:00 pm until 7:00 pm. This schedule was called "Two-a-Days", which lasted for two weeks, with the last day being a team scrimmage.

Before that scrimmage and two days before school officially started, I obtained a separated right shoulder during practice. This crushed hopes for improving the skills and techniques I had learned. Since my right hand was incapacitated by the shoulder injury, the world of art became like a distant memory. The academics course I navigated produced a disappointing and dismal first year.

Making a full recovery from my shoulder injury six months later, my determination to succeed never wavered. It only hibernated. Attending my first art class with all the confidence in the world was amazing and exciting. I was armed with some of my best creative works of art, and my enthusiastic creative human spirit, and I wanted to unveil these works of art to my professor. During that opening lecture, the professor asked if anyone brought any works of art to share with the class. I raised my hand and the professor walked over, took a drawing and painting from my mobile gallery. The professor had selected two of my most cherished pieces of artwork. The words that followed frightened me. "Your pictures look nice, but you have a lot to learn"! The words, "NICE", "NICE", "NICE" reverberated in my mind like vicious taunt, leaving me to doubt my entire self worth.

In spite of that comment, I knew that leaving college to return home was not an option. I thought to myself, there must be a way to succeed; I have been knocked down before and gotten up hundreds of times and I can do it again. Still dazed and stunned, while gathering some internal strength, I stood above my pictures which looked helpless below me. Just like a hungry bird of prey swooping down for a meal, I quickly grabbed the pictures and we flew towards the nearest exit.

Arriving at the dorms, sitting on my bed with the madness of my rapidly beating heart, the creative depth of my artful soul began blaming the non-creative years of high school for this embarrassment. Through my family's eyes, being the first to attend a major university or college, the heavy burden of beginning a family legacy generated energies of high brilliance of luster for finding strategic vessels for learning. My mission was the discovery and understanding new ways to augment my artful tools. It would prove to be a difficult decision, but I had to alter any previous strategies for learning to assure academic success. The uses of critical and creative thinking skills were essential to guarantee that these new ideas and constructs that were developed would essentially transmit academic success. Mark A. Runco (2003) defines:

> Critical thinking is the use of those cognitive skills of strategies that increase the probability of a desired outcome. This thinking is purposeful, reasonable, and goal-directed. Creative thinking refers to thinking that leads to an outcome that is novel (or unusual) and appropriate (or good) (p. 191).

I thought . . . . Wow! I knew what to do! I needed to have a rebirth in my approach for learning! I decided to focus on a pure art directed curriculum to be successful because, I was afraid to let go of the methodology of my way of learning and thinking. I knew that road to success would be tense and extensive but it was eminent. "A lengthy educational process is necessary before the raw intellectual potential—be it linguistic, musical, or logical-mathematical — can be realized in the form of a mature cultural role. Part of this process simply involves certain 'natural' processes of development, whereby a capacity passes through a predictable set of stages as it matures and is differentiated (Gardner, 1983). Consequently, this painful process, the key to beginning this rebirth was the preservation of my current knowledge. I viewed the process like this: Say, I have two large 8 ounce glasses, one filled with milk, the other a clear liquid. The glass of milk represented my prior and current knowledge and the clear liquid all of my professor's knowledge. With both glasses being full, the key to the rebirthing process was to pour all of my liquid from my glass. This was the one component that was frightening and difficult. It was a necessary ingredient for the transformation that would lead to new growth and understanding. Being open and receptive, I allowed the knowledge from the professors to fill my glass with their liquid of knowledge, concepts and artistic expression of art. At the end of each year I learned more concepts about art and how to apply them into other content areas. At the end of my forth year my glass became full with this crystal clear amazing liquid without any evidence of any murky milky residue! It was absolutely breathtaking and an incredible accomplishment to gain new knowledge and understanding with that kind of strategy. For the first time I felt good about being able to consent to those learning tools from the past.

"Understanding, or its opposite accompanied by feelings. There is the exciting "AHA" sensation of sudden illumination and the delightful feeling of "getting it" when understanding develops smoothly. There are feelings of bewilderment, confusion, and frustration, or sometimes instead feelings of wonderment and anticipation when we are confronted with something we do not understand" (Bereiter, 2002, p.113).

My shoulder injury in my freshmen year delayed the date of my graduation one semester. It was actually a blessing in disguise. In my sophomore year we won the National Championship as a Division II School. Football provided the only opportunity to attend college. It was a means, not an end, so I decided to place my football career on hold in pursuit of an all academic career. My coach took the news with sadness that my football career was over, but was proud to know I would continue to stay in school and get my degree.

The plan was to first complete my bachelor's degree by December, and second to apply to graduate school and receive my master's degree in Art by May of the following year. So, my academic world began. With only two classes to complete in the fall for my bachelor's degree, my application to graduate school was accepted as a concurrent student. This gave me the opportunity to continue and complete the second phase of my college career path. This was going to be the ultimate challenge; everything was in motion and visions of the realization of this plan are coming true. Graduate school would provide more deep-rooted insights for concepts, knowledge and skills to enhance my strong artistic abilities. In December of that year, the first phase was completed with me walking across the stage and receiving my Bachelor's of Fine Art.

While in graduate school, most of those classes were seminars, which allowed me to work independently for the preparation of the exhibition of my art works. It was a requirement to display levels of your artistic ability through physical productions and write a thesis on two major artists. The artists I wrote about were Leonardo Da Vinci and Michelangelo because of their abilities to incorporate the other core subjects, such as, math, science, social studies and language arts, enhancing their artistic abilities to create their masterpieces. Both artists influenced and supported my ideology of how art education should be part of the educational process in schools.

Most of my skills, concepts and knowledge were used to produce mainly paintings and drawings. Once a week my professors critiqued my artwork with positive comments. My chairperson would make the comment "I liked the painterly way you've painted those rocks", that meant he approved of my use of the paint on the paintbrush to create that object. With those kinds of comments, creating the kind of artwork that he would endorse was my motivating aspect to be creative. So, I sacrificed my desire to demonstrate my internal growth for external rewards. "On the other hand some artists might be prepared to sacrifice external effectiveness such as widespread public acceptance, popular admiration and high price in order to achieve internal effectiveness as they understand it ('authenticity', harmony among the painting's elements, innovative use of colour). This suggests that the two may sometimes be traded off against each other according to the priorities of a particular creator (Cropley 2001, p. 99).

The Gallery

With all courses in graduate school complete, it was time for an exhibition of my artwork which would be held in the University Art

Gallery. The public also was allowed to visit and view any exhibition on campus. The university mailed flyers for all art events welcoming others to experience new talent on the horizon. At the opening, my hair stood up on ends when hearing comments like, "Who is the artist? These paintings and drawing are wonderful!" Another comment was, "I would like to meet this artist!" "He's something special!" The success of my exhibition caused the university to change its policy on the length of time students can display an art exhibition. People requested the exhibition be displayed longer because others were coming from other universities to witness a fine display of talent.

The moment of truth had come. It was time for my committee to evaluate my exhibition. Since the responsibility of selecting professors was given to the student, choosing my committee members was an easy task. Most of the professors witnessed the evolution of change and knew of my hard work and dedication. Remember the professor who earlier had dismantled my paintings and drawing? He was part of my committee. After receiving excellent evaluations from each committee member on my exhibition and my thesis paper, walking across the stage in May, to receive my Masters of Art degree completed the second phase of my plan.

While walking on stage, the roar of the crowd became noticeably loud, so after shaking the last professor's hand, with my hands held high over my head, I walked to the edge of the stage. The crowd began screaming and yelling my name! After several minutes of a standing ovation, one of the professors tapped me on the shoulder. Turning to a wonderful smile the professor graciously escorted me off stage. That moment, too, will live on for the rest of my life!

Chapter II

THE ART REALM

After graduation and two years of working in retail industry in management, a teaching position opened at a boy's home in Detroit. The position required the applicant to have knowledge in Art, Industrial Arts and Math and submit a proposal for combining the subject areas. This miraculous opportunity would provide the perfect way to experiment with my methodology of teaching Art Education, if selected from the 150 candidates that applied. Following two weeks of interviews and anxious waiting, the Executive Director offered me the position during the final interview. I was astonished and grateful, as he produced a benefit package, employee handbook and keys after I signed the contract and other documents related to being employed at the boy's home.

After giving notice ending employment at my current position, top management tried altering my choice to leave by offering raises and incentives. I was curious, why top management made such wondrous offers for me to stay was baffling! Not until about a year later did the full meaning blossom. The government offered incentives in the form of tax breaks for those businesses with programs that promoted African-Americans to upper management. Soon that company folded, closing all its chain of stores in Michigan and across the country.

Operation Research

I took different routes driving to work. I drove past several half-burnt out houses and abandoned cars that sat on large wooden blocks with no wheels, which resembled huge empty lobster shells. Tall jungle size weeds covered two fields, which were on both sides of the street, displaying the tops of several unidentified objects in the distance. I thought that I had experienced and seen a lot, but this was an incredible sight to behold! Reaching my destination, the boy's home stood like a red brown brick castle surrounded by peasant dwellings, like that of old England. A large silver chain linked fence separated the manicured front lawn and playing field in the back of the home. Driving through the large side gates, I entered a long two lane jet-black driveway, which divided two buildings and led to a larger parking lot. To the left the main building, on the right side stood a small building where my classroom was located. That building was connected to the Gymnasium on the right.

Parking next to the entrance of my classroom had its advantages, especially escaping the sub zero weather conditions during those cold blistery days of winter. Trucks delivering equipment and supplies backed up to the door, easily unloading them. This large metal door, painted in dark pearl blue, had two dead bolt key locks with no windows. The classroom, being rectangular in shape, made it uncomplicated to arrange the equipment and furniture.

Inside the classroom, the walls were painted light pastel canary yellow, the floor a radiant polished white pebbled stone reflecting light from an eggshell white ceiling. The ceiling had lots of long tube bright Deco white florescent lights enclosed in a rectangular shaped clear plastic covering. Straight ahead, my metal fossil gray desk, with a matching cushioned wheeled chair, sat close by a phone mounted on the small wall. Following that wall around the corner, a long rectangular cactus green chalkboard with silver metal trim and chalk holder, which was mounted by silver brackets, almost engulfed the entire wall.

Using colored chalk I drew multicolored diagrammatic examples for lessons on the chalk board with such flare. The visual instructional aids resembled a painting that should have been framed! Facing the chalkboard were twelve large white pine-drafting tables, trimmed in light fog gray metal trimming, used by students. Arranged in three rows of four, each row, each table had a matching long four legged stool.

Behind the tables was a jet-black wide heavy chain linked door that led to a room, with one entrance and exit. This room was called the "cage". The cage stored all the classroom supplies and only with the permission of the teacher were the students allowed to enter. At the end of the cage was a wall with another gray metal door that displayed a red exit sign above. In close proximity near the cage and the back door stood an industrial size silver metal table top saw. The razor sharp circular blades would cut the large pieces of plywood with precision into smaller pieces, so as to make small furniture like tables and desks. Along the back wall, three mint-green lathes were angled towards the center of the room.

Against the next wall, which led you back to the front door, there were two mint—green disk sanders, a drill press and a walnut wood grained bookshelf. The bookshelf stored books about Industrial Arts, power tools and a how-to for staining wood. In the center of the room were two thick square industrial sized wooden top workbenches with four metal corner claps. The workbenches were mounted and secured on top of heavy-duty squared dolphin gray metal slabs, which contained small lockers for the boy's stored aprons and other equipment. The classroom environment was set up and ready to go. My task now was to implement my plan for "Operation Research"! That name was selected because of the structure of my program. As the boys learned Art Education, strategies were introduced adopting the learning cycles for integrating math; it was math applications and industrial arts in an industrial setting. For example, one learning cycle example was the introduction of two-point perspectives using the following steps: 1) Draw a box on the chalkboard. 2) Use certain measurements utilizing the mathematical equation $L \times W \times H$. 3) Review the application of using a ruler for measuring. 4) Explain the uses of power tools. 5) The final product led to the construction for a wooden bird house. How rewarding to see smiles on faces that once harbored looks of anger and despair!

Eventually, for inclusion into the public schools, the boys had to pass post written exams, in math, science, language arts and social studies, showing significant improvement and progress. This also gave them a measuring tool, and the confidence to compete with others their age and attend the nearest Detroit public school. With my innovative approach to learning, I've helped transform learning beyond the classroom into a real-world setting. I recall one boy in particular; let us call him Calvin, who entered into the program lacking the basic skills for learning, the tools and fundamentals for reading and writing. His world, at that time, was filled with drugs and alcohol, two parents who were unmarried and living in separate households, which gave him the opportunity to deceive both parents on his activities. Calvin was able to "run the streets", commit petty crimes, be arrested for those crimes and sentenced to a juvenile facility. He was "street smart", a smooth talker, and a very likeable and easily angered young man. He was released to the custody of the boy's home and his parents were stripped of their parental rights. Calvin quickly learned and understood how to apply my art education integration and how it has affected the way he learned in his other classes. His amazing increase proveniences in all of his core subject areas were recognized by other teachers at a staff meeting. The teachers commented and said they had noticed an unusual pattern in the use of drawings in his problem solving. I smiled, and then began to elaborate on my art educational drawing teaching strategies. The teachers listened very intensely while I explained Calvin's ability to use art education applications concepts and strategies in their subject areas. They all applauded! Calvin was recommended, by the staff to continue his education in a public high school setting, he was ready!

On his first day at school, Calvin's worst fear was that he wouldn't be prepared academically to compete with the other students. After being in a nurturing environment for one and half years, his reluctance to leave was more likely the case, later I found out this to be true. Once he conquered his fear, he soon realized that the learning strategies I taught him worked and became the cornerstone of his academic life. His teachers at his new school were just as amazed, too, by his unusual application of drawings for learning. He was the "Talk of the town"!

Calvin's academic success qualified him to attend a vocational school for metalsmithing. In class, he was always the first student to experiment with blueprints and schematics. He developed such an original way of thinking that he could draw a completed image from those blueprints for any particular product being made, with little or no directions. He soon became the teacher's apprentice, teaching those methods the teacher found difficult to teach the students. Calvin was one of twenty students to receive an internship at a Tool & Die manufacturing plant during his senior year, where he operated a lathe. The supervisor was, also, amazed at his abilities and skills and Calvin was given a certificate of excellence! After graduation, Calvin was hired by this company and placed in a management training program. He was the youngest person ever to be selected in that program. The last I heard, he was supervisor of one of those Tool & Die shops for that company. Other boys that graduated from the program at the boy's home occasionally visited and confirmed how the methods learned in my class helped them tremendously. More lesson plans will be discussed in Chapter Five.

For two years, Operation Research was very successful and delighted the Executive Director. Let me re-state the purpose of Operation Research. Operation Research was designed to provide an expressive and creative opportunity for experiences with art tools, concepts and skills with materials in a sequential process acknowledging the schematic development of student integration of the four core subject areas. The process would allow students to apply the elements and principles of design in a creative and unique way to solve or resolve visual problems. Was I trying to produce visual learners? Yes, Indeed! Other residential boys and girls home Directors heard about my program and visited and observed Operation Research with investiture of adopting a similar program. It was disheartening to feel the effects of the Reagan administration's proposal calling for the elimination of The Department of Education with other budget cuts that were associated within the education and welfare programs. Because funding for the educational programs at the home was allocated under a certain federal program, they had to reduce staff, eliminate one program, and refigure the home's budget. Being the last hired and thus the first fired, I tasted unemployment for the next two years. While collecting benefits from unemployment, I searched for other teaching positions without success.

The Awakening

Just as the unemployment benefits expired, a position for an Art Teacher became available at the Oak Park School / Ferndale District alternative high school located in Oak Park School District. After the second interview, the Director of the program pulled out an employee handbook, tax forms and a contract, and I was eagerly accepted as a "Para-educator". The school setting was similar to the structure of the boy's home in Detroit, the only difference being girls were enrolled. The director wanted the same kind of classroom application taught, but without the industrial arts portion. The students who attended this alternative school had violated school policies and had poor academic achievement. For the first two years, my methods of teaching art education astonished the director, teachers and students.

In my third year, science and art education was integrated into my curriculum. This was reminiscent of my time teaching at the boy's home, where my innovations for developing new strategies for teaching techniques and student learning began. For example, if they were studying the earth in science, my class constructed the earth using a round balloon, strips of newspaper, tempera paint and papier-mâché. The other subject area teachers soon duplicated was my interdisciplinary approach of systematically integrating art into the curriculum to ensure student learning. After my fourth year, a tenured teacher from Oak Park High School who had taught Social Studies replaced the retiring director of the program who taught math and algebra. Reviewing the information and notes from the previous director, the new director indicated that my teaching assignments would be art education, science, and math, including algebra. Teaching in the different subject areas gave me the opportunity to continue the growth and development of my cross curriculum teaching practices. I was more excited than Michael Jackson after he received his award for selling over twenty-five million copies of the album "Thriller"!

The Gift

Two years later, I received another opportunity to advance my teaching methodology from the Director of Oak Park/Ferndale Adult Education. The director, being familiar with my methods, offered me a substitute position teaching art in the evenings for a teacher who had taken a medical leave of absence at Ferndale High School. The director, pulling out a contract, emphasized the fact that my employment was as a "teacher" not as a para-educator and my pay would reflect that of a teacher! This magnificent window of opportunity created a unique privilege, a gift you might say, with the fortuity to experiment and develop my teaching practices and philosophy of Art Education with adult students.

The students in the program who attended my class were so excited and they appreciated the knowledge and learning environment. Their faces displayed a willingness and eagerness to learn more about the role of Art Education and its relationship to other subject areas. The class generated an energy that spilled down the hallway like hot molten lava pouring from a volcano. Even the director's visits were often and frequent, and the students enjoyed the interaction; some had never seen her prior to enrolling in my class. All of the students offered kind words about my teaching and threatened departure without me as their teacher. The director would tell the class not to worry.

When that teacher returned from sick leave, the director extended my employment retaining us both and offering two Art classes. Pre-registering for adult education was a prerequisite, and many of the new enrollees requested enrollment into my Art class, some even asking for me by name! Overall, enrollment increased that year and the director offered me other teaching positions in different subject areas such as accounting, communication, in addition to substitutions for other teachers.

After two more years of developing my teaching practices, the director of adult education resigned before the end of the school year. When the new director instituted various budget cuts, many teachers were reassigned and several classes were eliminated. One of them was my class and so once again, I was the last hired, the first fired.

Meanwhile, in the Oak Park Schools, budget cutting also eliminated programs district wide and the group most affected was the Para-educators.

Those without at least ninety credit hours or a degree from a college or university lost their positions or "bumped" other Para-educators with lesser seniority from their positions. Well, you know that being "bumped" is one thing, but being "bumped" into the SMI (severely mentally impaired) SXI (severely multiple impaired) program, at the Day Treatment Program, severely limited any and all thoughts or plans for fine tuning strategies developed from my adult education teaching experience in the different subject areas, including Art Education.

It takes a special person to work with this type of student and since my training with the special education population was zero, after thirty-three and a half long agonizing days, relief couldn't arrive soon enough. Other positions in special education SEI (severely emotionally impaired) LD (learning disabilities) were available and each position required the candidate to interview with the Director of Special Education. Out of twenty-five candidates, I was one of the four selected, and my classroom assignment was the lower elementary. At the end of that year, the programs moved into the Day Treatment Program in an elementary school building in Oak Park and then the director changed my assignment to upper elementary classroom.

Working with special educational students and staff, for the next six years, my appreciation, knowledge and skills developed. I learned how to modify art lesson plans for special education students with success. Just as I had done in college, I let go of some stored dormant strategies of the past and replaced them with innovative crystal clear liquid ideas. The director stopped into the classroom, on several occasions and observing my art lesson for the children thought the lesson were wonderful! On one of those days, the director pulled me aside, looked into my eyes and encouraged me to get a teaching certificate. This was my only option if teaching was to be part of my future. The director was using the Path-Goal Leadership Theory approach by Peter Northouse. Northouse (2001) writes:

> "In brief, path-goal theory is designed to explain how leaders can help subordinates along the path to their goals by selecting specific behaviors that are best suited to subordinate's needs and to the situation in which subordinates are working. By choosing the appropriate style, leaders increases subordinate's expectations for success and satisfaction (p. 90).

Following the director's advice, I registered at the nearby university in the teaching of Art Education. It required attending some daytime classes which meant that sometimes I had to leave my job early. Some of the other staff members voiced their opposition but the director told them to stop complaining and that the decision granting me permission to leave early was final. This situation created a lot of animosity among the staff, and transferring to another program or departing was the only cure.

In my final year at the Day Treatment Program, I applied for one of three newly created positions in computers opened to all the district employees. This was my opportunity to eliminate myself from this hostile environment.

Chapter III

NEW BEGINNINGS AND DISCOVERY

After three interviews with the Director of Technology / Data, I became one of three employees with the title of Computer Lab Technologist. My assignment was to create a learning technology environment at the middle school using three classrooms as computer labs, with thirty computers in each lab. For four years, the computer labs operated so efficiently that the structure for the middle school became the protocol operating system for the other computer labs in the district. Although I worked successfully with teachers in the core subject areas, I was exposed to several wonderful programs for art students.

Each core subject area program integrated cross curriculum learning with several art components. These programs were amazing! For example, there was this math program called "The Geometer's Sketch Pad". It assisted students in the creation of two and three dimensional objects. It also included the use of the five basic shapes (square, triangle, rectangle, cylinder, and circle) which art students could use for one and two perspective drawings. Unfortunately, any efforts to convince the Art teacher that technology should be part of the lesson fell on deaf ears.

During those four years, all of the requirements and tests needed for my teacher certification were completed. At the same time, the Art teacher at the middle school was reassigned to one of the elementary schools in Oak Park. The principal offered me the vacant Art position without any interviews, almost like being reassigned. This kind of decision made by the principal rekindled my confidence and my quest to apply my strategies of teaching art education.

Making the transition from a computer technology position to art education was difficult. My absence for actually teaching in a classroom was obvious as I found myself awkward in my delivery of instructions. My biggest challenge was making the students understand the difference between art and art education. Teaching sixth, seventh and eighth graders, in an African-American school culture, I discovered that my students required special treatment and different approaches. (These approaches will be discussed more in-depth in chapter IV).

The students regarded art education as one of those classes that had no meaning or affected their grades. They couldn't see the connection to real world applications, nor connect the knowledge learned to life experiences. I reassessed my strategies and began collaborating in writing lesson plans, in math, science, social studies and language arts. Knowing their lessons improved the writing of my own lesson plans, which enabled students to begin understanding and implementing tailored authentic assessments tasks in their assignments and projects. Using my eighth graders, I connected those assignments and projects to the world beyond the classroom. It allowed students to use varied techniques to create, construct and convey meaning through art education; expression of feeling, to persuade or communicate the knowledge and skills to influence an audience.

For example, I had the students create a children's storybook. Working in groups of three, each student was given responsibility for completing a part of the books. Their three choices were to be the Artist, Author or Editor. The characters and storyline had to be original with a lesson to be learned or another point of view. The lesson or point of view came from some past experiences with a current event or situation that had personal connection and meaning. Upon completion, students took their storybooks to an elementary school, in Oak Park, and read them to the children in the appropriate grade level. The use of Authentic Assessments was vital at this time. These assessments would substantiate or contradict my theory of how I'm teaching art education and the importance of this lesson.

The rationale for teaching this lesson: 1) Is this product (a storybook) a high-quality tool to use to measure students learning beyond the classroom? 2) Is this product sharing a way for students to achieve real-world experiences? 3) Could reading their storybooks give the students a different view of looking at how art education is being taught? 4) Would the students' self-worth for displaying and sharing their product with others be affected positively or negatively? Before the students embarked on their journey I gave the students specific instructions for classroom etiquette, including how to sit, how to call on students, and how to answer questions. Afterwards, I asked the students to meet in my classroom for lunch and for sharing and feedback.

When they returned from this experience, the expression on their faces was worth a thousand words! Expressions of joy, amazement and disbelief were apparent and I knew it was from the experience of reading to children and being the proud owner of a children's storybook. This was confirmed as we sat around a table eating lunch. I asked them these questions, "How did you like reading to the children"? All of them said that they really enjoyed reading their storybooks. "Were you nervous"? All of them answered by saying that they weren't nervous just excited! "Did you look at the children faces and into their eyes to discover that look of wonderment"? This one female student from the group, which there was four girls and two boys, said, "After I finished reading, I took the time to answer any questions and/or listen to comments from the children like you said". "This little boy was so elated that he wanted to know if I would take him home with me and read some more"! We all laughed! "Did you tell them that creating the book was a group project and explain to them your roll as the Artist, Author and Editor"? Again, the common response was, yes we did! The students also said, that most of the children expressed that they were looking forward to coming to my class so they, too, can create a storybook. After answering those questions with inspirational responses, each offered their services for future classes, if students did not want to read their storybooks. For all intents and purposes, each student conveyed their understanding of my approach for teaching art education. They articulated that my passion for art education was greatly appreciated and that their world has forever changed. This confirmed, with renewed vigor, my methods of teaching art education and helped reinforce strategies that I knew would be prosperous.

Not satisfied with winning the battle over how art education should be taught, conveying the idea of art education being part of the core curriculum, I felt it would be the ultimate challenge! However, before the grips of victory, strategic planning to take art education integration took the forefront, knowing this is only the beginning. There was lots of work to do. The need for someone to understand my teaching methodology and practices led to art educational workshops. During the summer month, while searching for assistance, I attended all kinds of Art Education teacher workshops in different school districts.

While attending most of the workshops, I discovered that each of them had a hidden agenda, advocating their own strategies of Fine Arts, not teaching practices for Art Education. The presenters were art teachers who talked vaguely about applying the other core subjects to art projects, yet no specific examples were shown or used to illustrate how they would be integrated into the lesson. The presenters would just say, "This art lesson can be used for science;" then the presenter showed the kinds of media used to make art projects and focused exclusively on the technical aspect of the art creation while ignoring the science aspects. Disappointed with the outcomes from my searches to find information or methodologies to enhance student's content area learning through Art Education, I felt unfilled and abandoned.

Two Sides of a Dream

I'll always be searching for that special person to share my world of a lively beautiful spectrum of colors, amazing warmth of passion and of breathtakingly splendor. It's a place I recommend highly! It dwells with dreams, flowing like a cool breeze on a warm summer night. It is also like the excitement of the "Grand Finale" at the Fourth of July fireworks celebration, and the magician who pulls the rabbit out of the hat! This place is my heart!

One hot summer, I attended a writing workshop. At that workshop, we were asked to bring personal artifacts that had special meaning, to class and share them. My thoughts were drawn to a Raggedy Ann doll that one of the female teachers had brought from home. Looking at the doll catapulted me back to the time of my youth. It was a time where poverty was like a gray, dark and foggy cloud that hovered over me everyday. The cloud of living in poverty did not allow avenues to encounter different adventures and privileges or access to expand my knowledge or to explore other environments. My existence was limited and linked to things being thrown away, hand-me-downs, gifts covered in dirt, discarded by someone not knowing that it had become a treasure for me. These items were musty; mud covered, amber yellowed, brown edged books, magazines and comic books.

Often, alone in my room, reading the stories took me to distant places and different times, and the foggy clouds of poverty changed into golden yellow sparkles of light and dust. After the golden dust settled, I wanted the dream to continue and be unbroken so my drawing skills would emerge. You see, drawing pictures prolonged my imagination. It gave me the power of flight and created an exodus from the world I lived in.

My cartoon characters were mostly of Superman, the man of steel, because flying with him made me feel protected and safe. At night, my dreams were flying without Superman. Flying alone, I usually flew to warm, tropical, beautiful islands where the aroma of sweet honey flowers embraced my senses.

Saturday mornings were the best times of all! All the television stations showed cartoons all morning. My interest and fascination was with one cartoon. I just loved, *The Raggedy Ann Show.* Raggedy Ann had a full head of dark curly hair, dark skin and patches all over her dress. Those kinds of patches were numerous in my family. She was always so happy, even though the patches on her shirt didn't match the patches on her skirt. Raggedy Ann had a friend, Raggedy Andy. He too, was always happy, had dark curly hair, dark skin and patches all over his shirt and overalls.

Identifying with Raggedy Andy made me believe that happiness came from within no matter what your clothes or hair looked like. Spending hours and hours drawing Raggedy Andy, with Raggedy Ann of course, I mentally placed myself into the laughter and fun they always had together. One day, seeing a colored picture of them both I received a very shocking discovery. Like a tire that had ran over a sharp pointed steel nail, the air slowly seeped out of the tire and my world began to sink. When the air had expired from my body, like the tire, it was my soul that had flattened with a sinking feeling. It sank deeply into the crushing depths of darkness of the ocean that destroyed my spirit. What a reprehensible deception! Raggedy Andy and Ann had red violet curly hair, not black; a dark apricot pink face, not dark brown skin; a carnation pink red nose and cheeks, not brown; strawberry red and white circled candy-stripped arms and legs, not dark gray; and their clothing was brand new with new patches, not old with stains or faded colors.

This further crushed my sense of belonging and justified my reasons to be alone. Our television set in those days, was a thirteen-inch black and white Motorola. I had never actually seen Raggedy Ann and Andy in color! They were not like me at all, "just some stupid cartoon, I thought! Nevertheless, using my sixteen-box of broken Crayola crayons, I colored the last two drawings of Raggedy Ann and Andy. As I looked at them, warm damp moist spots appeared on the picture. They were caused by a stream of cleansing tears running down both sides of my face; my heart just sank into the abyss of a black hole of an empty dream.

I gave those pictures away to end my devastation. However, seeing that Raggedy Ann doll at writer's workshop brought back my childhood memories and made me think how suddenly I longed to possess those pictures once again.

Now, looking back at my childhood I felt that other children around the world were just like me. They too had something that brought the world closer to them. After having that experience with Raggedy Ann and Andy the world became a much smaller place. Just knowing how difficult it was having only the bare essentials actually changed my vision of life. Being poor was not a curse, but a reality. How you deal with the cards you're dealt in life shapes you as a person. With my hands of cards, I have come to value the lives of all kinds of people, whether rich or poor, red, yellow, brown, black or white. It's the inner qualities and life experiences of a person that define, shape, and make them who they truly are. One way to measure this is to tell yourself it is not how much you love others, but how much others love you! Nevertheless, my fascination with drawing cartoon characters that could fly, like Superman, continued well into my teenage years. There were no comic book heroes who were from an African-American culture or of African descent; if there were some who could fly, they would be part of that special group. My main focus was to draw well enough so others could recognize the comic book character drawn.

The Butterfly

Today, this internalization has styled and shaped my personal works of art. Observing the creation of African-Americans as cartoons on television or comic book character heroes, like Blade who seeks out and destroy vampires and Cage whose super human strength fights crime in the ghetto from crime bosses, shows progress. However, my paintings and drawings are now all depictions of nature without the human figure. Removal of the human form became standard because of the disappointment of the Raggedy Ann and Andy travesty. My paintings reflect the jubilation of nature, mostly in seascapes. Colors have created my world of inspirations of regalement for the subject matter in all my paintings.

You'll find in all my paintings, aquamarine and turquoise blues, magic and electric greens, lemon and canary yellows mixed with ocher. You will also find splashes and sprays of titanium white waves, crashing against rocks or a shoreline, which engulf the canvas. I'm always flying into the settings or places in my paintings. The viewer experiences differences of passion. In one of my paintings, your view is near the mouth of a cave inside on the ceiling. From that ceiling you are looking down at waves smashing against rocks and watch those same waves carry white foam out to the sea. As you look outside the cave, that same wave joined another wave for a trip to shore. The colors are so breathtaking that you become tranquilized and your imagination frivolously takes control and transports you there, calm and content. During these tranquil moments, I envision and create new colors for my enjoyment of expressions.

Discovering and creating new colors when mixing on my palette, sings the songs of two lovebirds, and like a warm passionate kiss of two lovers, they were meant to be. Again, when viewing my paintings from a high vantage point above ground or higher places, these places are so very special when devoid of the human form.

Human figures create boundaries of incandescent expressions that limit the creative process; without them my painting becomes timeless. If you are on a pilgrimage investigating my paintings, through observation and discovery, you'll need an extraordinary invitation. Once invited, prepare yourself with a child's heart to permit you dispensation into a timeless place of beauty. You must be receptive to the floodgates of color, appreciate the wellspring of creative wonders of nature and enjoy the most precious gift that I could ever offer—my heart. I am thankful for just being alive and healthy.

Raggedy Ann and Andy came into my life as a child for a reason. The encounter emptied my soul and cocooned my body for years. Through time and knowledge, a metamorphosis occurred, rejuvenating my mind with understanding and wisdom and restoring my heart with charity and love. As an adult, passion fills my everyday existence. Helping others is automatic and giving love so freely without expecting anything in return, embraces my every thought. Raggedy Ann and Andy uplifted a child's world and dreams for a moment in time, making it real and believable. So, it does not matter to me now that the dolls were not African-Americans, only the fact they were part of my childhood fantasy.

Nevertheless, my efforts to sustain and perpetuate my childhood feelings of flying in the air, led me to scuba diving as an adult. Scuba diving, in the ocean, recreated and provided that same kind of flying environment in my dreams, not to mention the view. In the ocean's vast open spaces one can view a dancing magnificent spectrum of vibrant living colors. Submerged in the ocean, about 25 to 30 feet deep, the strong underwater current gently pushes the wonderful warm ocean water that surrounds the body. Stretching my body out into the crystal clear, sky turquoise, blue waters, I can fly and independently go wherever my heart desires.

Chapter IV

LITERATURE REVIEW

Failure of collaboration of common Art Educational Practices

While conducting my research and reviewing of the literature I found that there were no art education programs or organizations supporting my ideas for art education integration. The literature revealed quite the opposite. Even where art education was being taught all those schools, colleges, national and local art education organizations supported water down version of how art education is being taught. These three major areas emerged, Disciplined-based art education, current practices of the teaching art education and the use of technology in an art education classroom. These three areas will be discussed and summarize how these groups personalized their use of art education. In other word, I will attempt to examine and interpret the efforts these organizations tried to justify the funding from the major art education organizations like the Getty Foundation and the Getty Centers. I argue that art is not only important for its own sake, but is also a fundamental means through which students can learn the core subject.

Throughout the previous chapters you have been witness to my life's journey. You have examined my life experiences, explored how I improved of my current practices of the integrating art education and the teacher's role through personal narratives. It was designed to offer art educators insight into how a student's life learning experiences in his environment effects how the role of Art as an educational tool is used for integrating the four core subject areas.

It is my opinion that this is a critical area for decreasing the achievement gaps in urban schools. Art education integration could give urban schools an extra tool for increasing standardized test scores. University-based art educators need to know the students life experiences intersect cross curriculum learning and impact K-12 art programs in a variety of urban schools settings. University-based art educators are aware of the past years of art education that affected their field. The front runner of the most lasting changes that have affected the field of art education has been the Getty Foundation is discipline-based movement and the emerging of the electronic informational and technology movement.

Some art educators are utilizing technologies, like computers software programs, and internet integrating art education, are all outstanding. What is revealed is that art educators interpret the use of computer integration into classroom implementations and practices are acceptable tools for teaching art education. Those educators, who use computers, in fact try to personalize the use of computers in their classrooms. These educators do not realize, even with careful planning, how computers affect the hands-on experiences of the student. I agree with Maxwell (1996) who writes, "If your design decisions and data analyses are based on personal desires without a careful assessment of the implications of these for your methods and conclusions you are in danger of creating a flawed study" (p. 15).

At this point, it would be reckless of me not include literature that discusses different classroom practices being used in the teaching of art education. So, I must switch from a narrative to analytical social anthropological approach. Using the social anthropological approach Maxwell (1996) states that researchers employing the social anthropological approach usually are interested in the behavioral regularize of everyday life, language and language use rituals and ceremonies, and relationships. In order to provide a broad conjectural background for this study, the findings of the literature focused on three major areas:

Section I: The findings of the literature on discipline-based art education;

Section II: The findings of the literature of classroom practices; and

Section III: An examination of the findings of the literature on technology.

Finally, I will attempt to interpret how these three areas have created failure for integrating art education and make suggestions how to enhance the educational process in urban school settings. Using the interpretative approach Maxwell (1996) writes that this orientation allows researchers to treat social actions and human activities as text. This approach provides a means for discovering the practical understandings of meanings and actions.

Section I: Discipline-Based Art Education

Discipline-based art education (DBAE) can be traced back to Barkan's (1966) aesthetic education model that evolved through a long and slow evolution. This literature review will focus on the appearance of DBAE in the 1980s beginning with the Getty Foundation with the Getty Center's movement.

In 1982, The Getty Center for Education in the Art was created. The main focus of The Center was focused on issues that challenged art educators and those with decision makers. The Center's effort led to the adoption of a comprehensive art educational approach called discipline-based art education (Getty Institute, 1983). This approach became a common theme in art educational literature and published materials supporting DBAE.

Defining discipline-based art education. Discipline-based arts education is a comprehensive approach to instruction and learning in the arts, developed primarily for grades K-12 to provide exposures to life experiences and acquisition of content from four foundational disciplines of knowledge – production, criticism, history and aesthetics (Dobbs, 1998). It is the discipline of the art which provide the basic skills, knowledge and comprehension that engages students to have broad and life experiences with works of art. According to Dobbs, there are the four ways students to accomplish these tasks by doing the following:

- Creating works of art, through the skillful application of both experience and ideas, with tools and techniques in various media (art-making)
- Describing, interpreting, evaluating, and theorizing about works of art for the purpose of increasing understanding and appreciation of works of art and clarifying he roles of art in society (art criticism)
- Inquiring into the historical, social, and cultural contexts of art objects by focusing upon aspects of the time, place, tradition, functions and styles to better understand the human condition (art history)

- Raising and examining questions about the nature, meaning and value of art, which leads to understand about what distinguishes art from other kinds of phenomena, the issues that such differences give rise to, and the development of criteria for evaluating and judging works of art (aesthetics) (p. 1).

With urban school students, these four areas are inefficient ways to develop an interest in learning about art education or enhance their abilities to become learners. It isolates art education into an educational process entity of its own. DBAE theory resembles the thick white bubbly soap that drips down covering your windshield and windows at a carwash, impairing one's sense of directions and clouding one's sense of vision. It is my opinion that DBAE theory should be examining and exploring ways of how to integrate the four core subject areas (math, science, language arts, and social studies) into its art curriculum. The Getty Center called these four areas, art-making, art-criticism, art-history and aesthetics the four discipline of art education (Getty Institute, 1983).

Delacruz (1996) investigates the evolution of 14—year of the discipline-based art education (DBAE), an initiative introduction for reforming art education. The writers point out that aim at making education more su"stantive and rigorous and some efforts to address multiculturalism. Also, they aimed at the relationships "etween schools as public institutions, students with different learning and dIverse ethnic and cultural backgzounds have failed to produce any different approache3 to learning to those urban school students.

Basically, it continued to perpetuate the common theme of the four disciplines of art education. Day & Greer's (1987) justification for continu) ng using DBAE into four different defining characteristics: rationale, content, curricula and context. Clark and Geer wrote:

A) Rationale

1. The goal of discipline-based art education i3 to develop student's abilities to understand and appreciate art. This involves knowledge of the theorie3 and contexts of art abilities to respond to as well as to create art.

B) Content

1.
2. Content for instruction)s derived primarilx from the discipline of aesthetics, art criticism and art history and art production.

These disciplines deal with: (1) conceptions of the nature of art, (2) bases for valuing and judging art, (3) contexts in which art has been created, and (4) processes and techniques for creating art.

3. Content for the study is derived from a broad range of the visual arts, including folk, applied, and fine arts from Western and non-Western cultures and from ancient to contemporary times.

C) Curricula

1. Curricula are structured to reflect comparable concerns and respect for each of the four art disciplines.
2. Curricula are organized to increase students learning and understanding. This involves recognition of appropriate developmental levels.

D) Content

1. Full implementation is marked by systematic, regular art instruction on a district wide basis, art education expertise, and administrative support with adequate resources.
2. Student achievement and program effectiveness are confirmed by appropriate evaluation criteria and procedures (p.135).

Theses four defining (DBAE) characteristics conveys a continued deficiency of urban school student by creating other forms of art education in its definition, such as visual arts and fine arts, and recreating art as a specialized study, in its rationale. DBEA's implementation for teaching the study of Western and non-Western Art cultures are an undeserving approach, because it's teaching, to some extent, cultures that urban school students care absolutely nothing about.

While investigating how art education is used in the African-American culture for higher learning I found a different, but surprising, version of teaching practices for art education in Black Colleges. These institutions used more of a cultural visual art education curriculum.

Coleman (1994) used Black colleges and the development of African American visual as a tradition images of black's life countered negative stereotypes and that contributed what would become a familiar visual ethos of African American life. In other words, the Black college's use of art integrations took the outward appearance of reflecting its culture and its people rather than an integrated art education into the educational curriculum. Therefore, the content characteristics shortcoming is evident in this case. This can also be described as art appreciation curriculum. Integrating the curricula of the content from the four art disciplines will continue to disillusion the urban school students. To organize curricula to increase students learning and understanding will take more than just the recognition of appropriate developmental levels.

The intrinsic value of art study, discussed by Coleman (1994), traced the development of African-American visual arts tradition with Historically Black Colleges and Universities (HBCU) contributes to institutionalizing. Many of these black colleges, with the assistance of white philanthropists and black organizations, were financed and built. African-American colleges engaged in continuing the past foundation of art concepts and folklore through visual arts, in order to ensure that separation existed between art and the content areas. In a state of frozen animation, images of black life centered on learning from one aspect of art education. Instituting changes at the HBCUs, in its programming for art education, many would suffer the consequences of not being funded. So, few HBCUs won't introduce new concepts or theories deviating from the norm. This threatens African-American students' uses of higher order thinking, learning how to learn and expansion of supplementary at the forefront into any innovative progression of art integration. The Getty Centered Foundations have created and provide grants and scholarships funding for those schools who have adopted their theory and practices of art education. Awards are given to teachers who teach DBAE in their classrooms. For example: Mrs. Cary Schott was the recipient of the Annenberg / Getty Grant, she also received the Florida Elementary Art Teacher of the Year 2000 award.

In the Florida school system each school practiced its own form of art education, display and promoting dissimilar kinds of art curriculum. Within the context characteristics, how can there be a full systematic "regular" art instructions implemented on a district-wide basis when different theories are being taught. How can student achievement and programs effectiveness be confirmed by appropriate evaluation with different areas being assessed, visual arts, fine arts and art education? It can not provide any authentic assessments with some degree of accuracy leading to the development of quality art education curriculum.

The National Art Education Association organization supports DBAE NAEA advocates, not only the theories and practices of DBAE, the adaptation of *National Visual Arts Standards* (2003). One policy separates distinctions between the Getty Centered Foundation and National Art Education Association for receiving awards, grants and scholarships.

With the NAEA one must become a member of the foundation, must pay and maintain current yearly membership dues to receive any awards. Foundation grants are awarded to members only. Their efforts seem to be more political in nature and exhibit more of a rallying cry "to arms" for the protection of their own agenda or cause as stated in their booklet, *Where's Art Now? Support Improving Art Education Policies* (2002). With fees assessed, urban schools can not afford to allocate funding from the budget supporting that type of an expense.

The National Board for Professional Teaching Standards (2002) supports DBAE with their report *Early Adolescence through Young Adult / Art Standards, Second Edition.* They write:

> Accomplished teachers, exhibit general and content-specific knowledge and skills in art making, art criticism, art history and aesthetics. They have a solid grounding in the forms, theories, philosophies, forming processes and contexts of art. Fundamentally, they know how to study, interpret and evaluate works of art; know how and why works of art are created; know how to organize and teach the content of art; and particularly, know their students and students' developmental needs (p. 38).

Clearly, (DBEA) intentions were misleading here because their effort shows their implementation dose not focus on the student's learning abilities, but instead focus on the implementation of the development of teachers' strategies for teaching. The article never states the process by which teachers can assess their students to determine developmental levels. With urban school students this assessment, if not administered correctly, could have an adverse effect on the students' learning and achievement. The dishonesty comes from the teaching of African-American students about making art, art history, and art criticism and art history of artist who are not African-Americans. These artists have no significant meaning to their culture or way of life. They are being taught that this is the only way to learn about art education.

The literature branched of into many directions. My question at this point, "How does the US Department of Education view art education?" "Are there any standards or goals for the teaching of art education integration?"

Riley (1994), National standards for arts education part of *Goals 2000: Education American Art, the Clinton Administration's plan for nation education reform,* gave this report. The report endorsed by Riley, U.S. Secretary of

Education, outlines the standards outcomes of what ought to learn in music, theater, dance and the visual arts, with proposed standardized testing in each area. Mr. Riley's outline for elementary and high school students continues to separate and renames art education into the visual arts, with no mention of middle school students. To propose standardized testing is innovative, with different approaches and philosophies in teaching, the problem of how teachers demonstrating a comprehensive understanding of the essential knowledge, concepts, skills, methodology and processes that compose the content of art education to teach universal theories and practices across the nation. This is the first time a U.S. Secretary of Education has purposed any kind of standardized testing for the arts. As Zimmerman (1990) points out:

> Art teachers across the United States continuously face the problem of how to educate students to learn about art in all cultures contexts. They also must adapt teaching strategies, curriculum content, and learning environments to best meet individual students' needs. Solutions to these problems involve issues such as changing ethic and cultural forces in the United States, debate about elitist populist view of art education, value of an "aesthetic" or "cultural" approach to studying art objects, and appropriate, equitable strategies art teachers can take to educate students from a variety of background (p.185).

With funding for art education, some schools developed strategies for securing grants and scholarships, advocating and emphasizing sections of DBAE theories and practices. Some private schools submit applications for funding as well.

Nelson (2001) how the Oxbow School in Napa, California is a one-semester fine-arts boarding school for high school students with equal facility in academic as well as artist fields in order to promote multidimensional creative thinking. This project was the conception of Ann Hatch, founder of San Francisco's Capp Sti Project that began in September 1999. The 16-week curricula were geared mostly to academic, lectures, workshops, and community-based experiences. It gives students training in visual arts with ties to future environmental beautification of their communities. Finished projects are displayed at public receptions.

This boarding school use visual art as tool for measuring the success of the program to the public. Using the DBAE of art making funding for this project continued from public support and other art foundations. Furthermore, this approach advocated multidimensional creative thinking instead of art education. Dowd (2002), and *"Organizing Art Work"* writes:

Some basic methods for organizing our notions of art activities can be identified by examining changes with art's historical means-of-production, ideological, economic, and modal divisions. Alternatively, the artist curriculum could be organized, based on modes of artistic thought and function, into five categories: constructors, theoreticians, storytellers, visual rhetoricians, or visual analysts (p.14-19).

It is my conviction that the content of this paper divides art education into areas of philosophical entities instead of integrating art education in the four core subject areas. All of the basic elements of DBAE are evident, but the renaming continues. Scheinfeld & Steele (1995), *"Expressive Education: arts-integrated learning and the role of the artist in transforming the curriculum"*, funded by The Erikson Institute Art Projects operating in the Chicago public schools writes:

The structures of most successful arts-integrated lessons follow a regular pattern: A focal subject matter or concept provides the stimulus; the integrated lesson joins language, thought, and art in an interpretive process related to this focal point. The lesson itself is organized around the artistic process, involving the interaction of four modes of action: playfully responding to stimuli, transforming them into inner imagery, expressing the imagery through artistic work, and evaluating the expression (p. 22-27).

These kinds of strategies take away a clear direction for teaching the students art education integration and instead focus one aspect of art, which is expression. Milbrath (1998) points out:

When children are made to focus on certain aspects of a model, they can use strategies that clearly differentiate the views of the presented model. A key point made by all is that production decisions made early in the drawing determine the direction a drawing takes (p. 29).

In effect, creating art education learning with patterns dealing with the language of interpretive processes will undoubtedly artistically disillusion urban school students with confusion of concepts needed to interpret the lesson being learned. The several methods of action seem to transfer the curriculum in an aesthetic integration, not art education integration, in DBAE. Students are searching for concrete and solid guidance and directions for learning art education concepts and skills. Failure of the teachers to provide structured strategies could render art education ineffective and dangerous if students and left to their own devices for learning through interpretation of lessons presented. These lessons resemble visual-spatial art by allowing the student's visual expressions for learning. This definition was presented in 1984 by Howard Garner's book, *Frames of Mind: Theory of Multiple Intelligences.* Gardner wrote:

> While one might underestimate the component of spatial thinking in the sciences, the centrality of spatial thinking in the visual arts is self evident. Thus, an individual with strong abilities in the spatial realm should learn to recognize target patterns quite quickly when exposed to them, to appreciate their identity even when their arrangement in space has been altered and to notice slight deviations from them when they are presented on subsequent trials or subsequent days (p. 195-200).

Transforming students' performances to achieve such advances skills, concepts and knowledge, the teacher expertise must be in philosophy not art education. With urban students, this kind of setting will initiate negative discipline classroom behavior. In other words, African-American students need more structure. Art educators controlling discipline problems are by far an enormous challenge on a daily basis. Diverse ethnic and cultural students confront teachers with insurmountable conflicting needs and divergent values. Other factors associated with classroom management are complex and difficult to control. The delivery of instructions creating a learning environment must be adequate (Susi, 1990).

Another noticeable area the literature highlighted was in the directions of humanities. This version of art education application is far removed from the concepts of art education integration. Its version is more of a scholarly approach than teaching art skills or concepts.

Another area the literature highlighted was in the area of humanities. This version of art education is far removed from the concepts of art education integration. In 1991, Levi & Smith wrote about a humanities-based conception of DBAE. Levi wrote:

> The humanities cannot be dismissed. Far from being outmoded, they are externally relevant because they are the arts of communication, the art of continuity, and the arts of criticism. Philosophic criticism is the only activity through which man's self-reflection modifies the conditions of his existence. The cup of the humanities, therefore, must be the vessel from which we drink our life.

In the definition and practices of The Philosophy of Art Education, many art teachers develop a formal statement originally, and then continue to use that same philosophy as current practices teaching in the classroom without modifications. Rockman (1999) writes, "They learn, as I have learned, to embrace the unfamiliar as an opportunity to grow, to be challenged and driven ahead by what they do not know rather clinging solely to comfortable and familiar experience." (p. 3)

Undoubtedly, this movement reflects not just separation, but total annihilation of art education. In his view, art is regarded as a tool by which to assist the indispensable medium of language and breathe of history that provides group memory which bonds people together. That man's creative nature is inspired by the historical content, controlled internal environments, not concepts of learned knowledge and skills, nor integration of art education into the four core subject areas.

Finally, Delacruz (1996) examines the evolution and controversy following the introduction for art educational reforms of DBAE and attempts to conveyable of accepting practices by considering differences in context and introduction of DBAE paradigm, with the future and professional concerns related to the integrity of The Getty Center.

Summary. In the findings of the literature, discipline-based art education (DBAE) is not widely accepted as a universal way of teaching art education; however, it is an important educational model that benefits the visual arts in non-urban school setting. An art educator struggles with different constructs and conceptual strategies for urban education for years. Failure to justify art education into the curriculum is not unusual or uncommon (Simpson, 1995). Discipline-based art education, for all practical purposes, was the creation of the Getty Center for Education in the Arts. Subsequently, many art teachers view the DBAE as the "chimera" includes "an imaginary monster amalgamated of incongruous parts "unrealistic dream" and even some the "Holy Grail" for art education (Hoffa, 1990). Those who followed the practices and theories of the DBAE where treated like heirs born with silver spoons in their mouth. If those who support DBAE begin to recognize the racial bias of these four disciplines and consequently teach outside them, practicing these discipline will cease.

DBAE is impregnated with humanity's most treacherous atrocities – racism (Fehr, 2000). Fehr argues by not extending invitations to any urban schools to participate in the development of DBAE, theories and practices are academically reckless and culturally arrogant.

The National Art Education Association (NAEA) political platforms, art educational policies and agenda is to clearly reward paying members only with certain rights, benefits and privileges for being a member. Its only function is creates a national review of how art education policies can enhance the quality of art education for teachers, then the student.

The finding of the literature supports the notion of DBAE theories changed the art educational experiences and could have developed in spread wide practices. The issue centering on urban schools have limit or deny diverse content inclusion. The next section of the literature review will explore classroom teaching practices in an art education.

Section II: Classroom Practices

Barnes (2001) describes making links between principles and practice, traditionally, have proven difficult. Art teachings have continued apparently vague and random objectives still characterizes a majority of classrooms. Barnes argues that teachers should make connections for themselves but that would be to ignore problems of putting theory into practice. With and understanding of principles, the defining point of any theory, does not guarantee or lead to excellent practice. Excellent practice does not insure that principles of teaching art are comprehended.

In the late 1990s, the Discipline—based art education (DBAE) for reforming art education by the Getty Center to develop students abilities to understand and appreciate art and instructions derived primarily from four discipline of aesthetic, art criticism, at history, and art production. The concept provoked a divisive national acceptance of how art education shaped current practices taught in art education classrooms.

Barnes believes that art for children can be a vessel whereby they recreate and assimilate experiences they have had. Incomplete inner vision can crystallize enough for meaning what they encounter and assisting in the building of concepts of themselves in juxtaposition to the world. This section of the review will explore art educational processes of classroom practices.

Classroom instructions and practices. At this point, the literate led me towards how certain cities introduce art education integration in urban schools. Upon reviewing closely, the literature focused on the city that gave the impression of teaching featuring some art education activity was in Chicago. The urban schools in Chicago use Teaching Artist (TA) to teach art education. I reviewed several kinds of different literature that supports TAs in the Chicago schools. Analyzing these articles, I will make comments with my concerns of how the Chicago school, using this method of teaching students art education in an urban setting, have short changes the process of learning for those students.

Lynn Waldorf (2003) examines the *Chicago Arts Partnership in Education* (CAPE) Summer of 2001. One hundred and fifty Teacher Artists (TA) who had worked for the partnership in the Chicago's urban schools K-12 classroom, congregated for sharing goals and experiences. These goals divulged a holistic approach to artist influences, well beyond basic teaching specific art skills or concepts in the classroom. Waldorf writes:

> This study influenced CAPE to focus on teacher training as major aspect of its educational mission. In addition, although the general goal of lesson planning was to integrate the study of an art form with enriching comprehensive in other areas of the school curriculum, twenty-seven percent of respondents listed the development of basic learning skills, such as listening, analyzing and conceptualizing as a common objective (p. 13-18).

Burrows (2003), "A Teaching Artist", writes:

> A Teaching Artist assumes the mantel of a broader experience. Artist who teach primarily teach from their own experiences, their own life or their own professional processes. A Teaching Artist primarily offers opportunities for other to make entry into the creative, artistic, historical and aesthetic experience of the arts (p. 7).

Booth (2003) *is* seeking definition and practices of Teaching Artist discovered that their curriculum is driven by placing artist at the center of learning. According to Waldorf (2003), TA's interest was to effect the social-cultural aspiration in students population in high poverty urban areas, promoting democratic educational principles of equity, diversity, self-respect and construct collaborative skills to promote a sense of a learning community. Booth (2003) promoted the use of TAs and thought that the approach was innovative. Of course, my position is for teaching art education integration in urban schools, which differs from and do not share his reasoning for this kind of approach.

Paulson (2003) states that sentiments of Teaching Artist became conscientious of their practices and asked how to prepare for teaching. The question was asked *"Where can I find out what the expectations are for teaching the arts in the classroom of K-12 school"?* (p. 45). The response question here is *"Who are they asking"?* The controversy of TA's assimilates one universal theme taught in the classroom, they regressed back to their own work. This regression effect was mainly, I believe, due to the lack of courses in the college of educational at a major university or college.

The literature referred to the world of arts and craft as another method of teaching art education.

Backer (2002) examines arts and craft education centered around the country's youth. He writes:

> That despite the positive climate for the arts education in America, fears have been expressed over the effects of the *No Child Left Behind Act*, which passed in January of 2002 places additional focus on math and science in America's elementary and secondary schools.(p. 22-28).

This kind of legislature passing into law, does not focus on developing an universally understanding of art education, the value of art education or how art education contributes to the four core subject areas.

Collins (2001) discusses interactive art education he writes:

> Unique attempts at true interaction have been developed by artists who address such issues as user-control process. Attempts of this kind suggest approaches to interaction that could be employed for diverse types of learners in various educational settings (p. 19-21, 60-61).

Collins suggests that for diverse type of learners the acquisition of interaction learning is the best practice, not integration of concepts and skills into the core subject areas. This kind of methodology using TAs devalues art education as a subject, which gives the impression that anyone can teach art education as long as they have some affiliation with the subject of art. Using TAs will continue separating the art from art educational integration process. This seems to be the only way that art justification is support and funding by school districts, without realizing the consequences of their actions.

Hoppe (1995) scrutinizes a special role in art education despite widening gaps that appears to subsist amid the avant-garde and the arts education movement. The writer argues, through a combination of factors and situation, indicates a new arena for teaching art education activities of the American avant-garde definitely be taught in public schools in the nation. The factors that he speaks of are how art education is introduced into public schools. The situation is the use of TAs seems to be the new way of teaching art education. This group or movement has labeled themselves postmodern re-constructivists. Postmodern re-constructivists have been demanding acceptance of a new paradigm for avant-garde practices, instead of art integration. These reconstructivists would place outside acceptance the realm of art educational contexts and consign non-interconnecting teaching with the emphasis towards social responsibility for art education. He continues the argument that arts educators in the United States and in a foreign country have been formulating principle for innovative pedagogy, stressing collaboration comparatively more than competition. The dissection and restructuring of art education, viewed through the reconstructive postmodern theory lens, advocate a new-era classroom for schools and the educational system are prepared for consideration of this progress as artistic quality for teaching art education. It is my belief that, placing avant-garde as practice in art education becomes an additional philosophical way of creating another amplified attempt to create an altered state of teaching art education and undermine any integration transversely into the educational curriculum. In other word, these postmodern theories go against my belief that teaching art education should be taught in the classroom, across the curriculum and not across outside social applications.

Gude & April (1995), Arnold April, Executive Director of the Chicago Arts Partnership in Education (CAPE) and Olivia Gude, a Chicago-based artist specializing in collaborative effects creating public works of art, converse about why art occupies a subordinate position within primary and secondary education. They both argue in support of the use of TAs and that the potential for using TAs to teach art would increase the participation of urban school students in art, making them have rich learning experience in art not art education. They also discuss that this method is very challenging for teaching art, but do not offer any alternatives. My major concern is that the CAPE program are filled with motionless theory and practices that focuses on and encompasses artist not teachers. The failure to substantiate and adopt the precise role of TA's is reason why art in the public schools, in Chicago Urban schools are positioned in a subordinate position for educating students.

Establishment of the National Art Education Association. This section of the review deals with the establishment of the NAEA beginning for Teacher Preparation. The original guideline for art teachers' preparation programs were formulated by a commission of the National Art Education Association (NAEA) in 1970 and revised and disseminated as standards in 1979. Art teachers' preparation programs were designed to provide students (Teachers) with strong backgrounds of learning the in art education and the visual arts. Course work is structured to develop expertise in studio art, art history, art criticism and aesthetics. Art teacher candidates obtain extensive preparation to deliver comprehensive instructions helping students create, study, interpret and evaluate works of art (NAEA, 1985). *The National Visual Art Standards* emphasized what every American student should know the following:

1. Be able to communicate proficiently in the visual arts.
2. Develop and present basic analyses of work of visual art.
3. Have informed acquaintance with exemplary works of art from a variety of cultures and historical periods.
4. Be able to relate art knowledge within and across the art disciplines (NAEA, 1994, p. 14).

Educational leaders began recognizing that teachers were the means to educational reforms. This was considered the most significant and optimistic events in recent years in the development of national standards for certification by the *National Board for Professional Teaching Standards* (NBPTS, 1994). These voluntary standards permit excellent teachers to demonstrate professional strengths developed by experiences, advanced study, and thoughtful practice. The standards are based on five extensive propositions with reference to teaching:

1. Teachers are committed to students and their learning.
2. Teachers know the subjects they teach and how to teach those subjects.
3. Teachers are responsible for managing and monitoring students learning.
4. Teachers think systematically about their practice and learn from experience.
5. Teachers are members of learning communities (NBPTS, p. 1-3).

In the NBPTS publication (1994), *Early Adolescence through Young Adulthood/Art: Standards for National Board Certification*, establishes lofty standards for what teachers should know and understand, certifying teachers who meet those standards and to improve learning in America schools.

Art Education had transformed in the last two decades that the *NAEA Standards for Art Teacher Preparations* have been revisited with mindful efforts to reveal the reality of current art classroom (NAEA, 1994, p. 14). The reexamination of those inventive standards in the context of current thinking and practices was convened to instigate the process as part of the NAEA initiative concerning art teacher preparation by a committee in September of 1996. The revised standards were dispersed to the membership and presented to the NAEA Board of Directors for approval in 1999.

Criticisms of NAEA Standards for Art Teachers. So, how did the field of art education receive NAEA Standards for Art Teachers Preparation when it first appeared? Each state adopted segments from the standards to create their own version for classroom art teachers, similar to the sculpting away of DBAE into current practices and altering art education into the visual arts, for most states. In a 2001 publication from the state of North Carolina, where the Department of Public Instruction have implemented the K-12 visual arts program in the public school, it states:

> The visual art seeks to provide visual literacy for every child by promoting fluency in modes of visual communication to include studio production, art history, aesthetics and criticism. Students learn the characteristics of visual art wide range of subject matter, media and means to express their ideas and knowledge. They evaluate the merits of their efforts and this assessment forms the basis for further growth that extends to all disciplines in school life in general.

In a 2000 publication from the Idaho State Board of Education, Standards for Visual Arts Teachers, again art education has been reconfigured so that Art Teachers should:

- Have an understanding of the history and foundation of arts education
- Have a thorough understanding of the process and content of the art discipline being taught.
- Understand the aesthetic and artist purposes of arts.
- Understands how to explore philosophical and ethical issues relative to the arts.
- Recognizes how his or her art content relates to the lives of students and the educational community in which he or she teaches.
- Recognizes that learning about art and creating art are enriched by opportunities to attend and respond to art exhibits and performances and that these opportunities are an integral part of the arts curriculum.

Hanson (1994) writes:

> The effectiveness of art education in California schools does not depend entirely on the subject matter preparation of art

teachers. Another critical factor is the teacher's ability to teach art and to address the pedagogical knowledge and effectiveness of art teachers. The new program standards are closely aligned with the state-adopted content standards for students; as a consequence, they strengthen the visual arts K-8 classroom. The Content Standards for the Visual Arts was adopted in 2001. These new credential requirements reflect the need for greater breadth and depth in knowledge in the core subjects including the arts.

As a consequence, the Commission will implement an original examination called the California Subject Examinations for Teachers (CSET). This examination over the next four years, replace the current SSAT and Praxis II subject area exam. The CSET developed exam with be administered by National Evaluation System, Inc., scheduled in January 2003.

With the adoption of most states NAEA standards and implementation of revised examination for art teachers, both seem irrelevant and potentially oppressive to urban school students since urban schools were denied an invitation during the assemble of the commission. Ross (1994) writes:

> Regrettably, these sums up the problem with any set of standards, and most poignantly, with those proposed for the arts education. Even though some of the standards are written in a way that recognizes the necessity of view growth in the arts by levels rather than by arbitrary expectations by grades, even those are not attainable in the majority of U.S. public schools. What might have been an eloquent statement of expectations and how they are to be achieved is little more than a restatement of ancient goals and objectives more appropriate to the United States of 1950 Hollywood movies (p. 26).

Paulson (2003) discusses that this topic is a new publication and a resource for state dialogue, released in June of 2002, outlines the requirements for all new teachers should know, be like and able to accomplish to teach education effectively (p. 45).

With urban schools being denied representation or suggestions for making decisions creating art educational process and policies, which is led by a non-legislative body of art educational organizations and schools, is one thing, but it seem to me that they are questioning the competencies of the teachers abilities to teach urban school students art education effectively. Rusch & Thomas (1990) answer the question. Thomas discusses the question of whether or not the existing population of art teachers is prepared to teach the NAEA essential components of aesthetics, art criticism, and art history and art production. In fact, numerous teachers are prepared; the predicament is how to make it perceptible. The NAEA essential components guilds their own practices. The process focuses, of self-evaluation, on using three or four components, aesthetics, art criticism and art history, since these are most questionable in regards to preparedness of teachers' practices in the classroom.

Finally, the NAEA and other Art Association groups continue using urban schools as testing grounds for the development of new ideas for teaching art educational teaching practices. Once these practices are fined tined, these practices are utilized in other school districts. With this kind of practices the learning of art education in urban schools will be devalued, placed on individual art education organizations policies whose interest lies in self edification. The insufficient progress has been made in recent years improving schools preaches innovation. District across the nation continue with reforms based on higher levels for accountabilities, site-based management, learning standards, basic skills curricula and will the reforms provide the framework for educational programs address the needs of all students (Lewis, 2001).

The literature also takes a look at established art schools in the across this nation view of art education. These institutions concern for art education integration is not at the forefront, but are struggling to restructure their approach towards students learning art education by using a different version of art education. Their approach to teaching art education is social intended with emphasis placed more on cultural aspect then educational.

Nestor (1996) discusses the developing relationship of their facilities and activities of art schools towards the students' ability of quality art-making rather than students' art education learners. He suggest the difficulty for making art schools a more creative environment must shift form preparing future artists would be considered as innovations in the institutions art education curricula. This kind of transformation is creating a crisis for the survival because of limited resources and funding.

According to Gregg (2003), after seventy years since the first art degrees appeared, art-schools have reexamined their missions and values. It's difficult to determine the best practice to use the short time allocated for art degrees. Gregg writes:

An undergraduate fine-arts major frequently spends just one of his or her four of years in art classes, and even a two-year master of fine arts program does not allow much time for training, compared with the decades in art-school conference rooms countrywide are the proliferation of programs and students, the embrace of diverse art forms and content, the professionalization of art practices, the rise of cultural theory, whether and how to teach the new technologies that have appeared in the last decade, whether to teach particular artisanal skills, and even the very definition of art (p. 106-109).

Jenkins (1986) inspired by Lowenfeld & Brittain attempts to help clarify any confusion between the Philosophy of Art Education and The Philosophy of Fine Arts:

Philosophy of Art Education	*Philosophy of Fine Arts*
Emphasis is on encouraging creativity regardless of where it is used.	Emphasis is on the aesthetic value of the end product.
The creative process is most important.	The final product is most important
Art is used as language	Art is used as art form
Emphasis is on sensitive viewing visual literacy.	Emphasis is on doing; making
Feelings behind the work are most important	Aesthetic appearance is most important.
Encourages experimentation with materials.	Encourages training and techniques.

Jenkins initiative failed to develop a universal fundament language, with inadequate support, the art associations ignore and proceeded to implement standards and language.

One the other hand, Jenkins definitions subsequently fail to address the integration of the four disciplines in art education, which from this viewpoint, still continue to inequitably present art teachings and classroom practices. A definition of the

Philosophy of Art Education, from a personal view point, is implemented with this approach:

- Emphasis is on encouraging creativity; how it is used and the end product.
- The integration process of the final production is important.
- Art is used as a discipline.
- Emphasis is on integrating the four disciplines.
- The connection or links are most important.
- Encouraging fundamentals of techniques using the four X's of learning (examine/exploration/experimentation/expression).

From these fundamental structures, the complexity for understanding the definition of the Philosophy of Art Education, may perhaps, activate a common classroom practice and theory for art teachers nationally. Efland (2002) writes:

> I called attention to this developmental tradition because it has profoundly imposed a long-standing mind-set within the culture of practice in art education, where the best teaching is thought to be no teaching at all, and where artistic accomplishments are judged primarily for their therapeutic rather than their education value. Such long-standing historical biases have made it difficult to recognize the study of art as a cognitive endeavor. (p. 48-49).

Teachers, who support a broad approach to learning about art, supporting the two, Philosophy of Art Education and Fine Arts, transmit art programs with different approaches that adversity effects student learning. Jarvis, Holford & Griffin (1999) write:

> Rather, we now think of learning as a social activity. Learners learn when they engage with knowledge in social contexts. If we take this view, it is apparent that "learning" is likely to vary, depending on where, how and why it is taking place, and who is doing the learning. This represents something of a challenge to traditional views of learning and teaching, where the quest has too often been for the "theory of learning" (p. 66).

There has been much attention, by educators and other organizations, which have advocated changes of the art educational practices and policies for teaching art education. It is my belief, those changes of practices and policies involving urban schools have been indistinctly misrepresented and that quality of art education is far below standard. Cornbleth (2000) writes:

> I have noted cross-currents and describe the resulting tensions within and among curriculum politics, policy and practice. These cross-currents are endemic in the U.S. as conditions, interests, and political coalitions change. Curriculum is continually contested, and both curriculum policies and practices are not only made, but unmade and remade by numerous and unofficial education policymakers and practitioners (p. 234).

Summary. The findings of the literature reveal certain aspects of ambitious adopted state and local policies with regard to current practices teaching art education in the classroom are non productive. The language of the new federal legislation, No Child Left Behind is aimed at creating an additional inflexible certification for teachers. Many states are reviewing their teacher preparation requirements to guarantee conformity with the new law. What constitutes a qualified teacher is currently an enormous question. Urban schools are just scrambling for academic acceptance, a right to be heard and to develop an educational partnership in determining and developing curriculum outcomes. Upon examination of the adoption of national standards and curricula, Cornbleth (2000) argues that such a development displays efforts of cultural containment.

Implementations of this teaching approach, without structure in an urban school art education classroom will continue to create handicapping conditions that limit or deny integration of the four disciplines. This statement implies that an immense transformation needs to be completed to offset the insufficiency of current cultural teaching practices. In other word, urban schools need to take charge of their own art educational curricula and place no faith within the national or local art advocates who adopt their own policies.

The literature presented deteriorating ineffective art educational teachers because of the lack in monitoring or mentoring the experiences for the duration of their preparations for teachers. It is my belief that the art education teachers were not ineffective, but rather was confused on how to teach art based education to urban school students. With the Department of Education, national and local art organizations all making different policies and practices, teachers do not know what exactly to teach or how to teach it. These policies are supposed to reshape art education into receptive practices that all art education teachers can teach in their classroom. It is essential that the art education curriculum reform include contributions from diverse constituencies, which includes urban schools, to unify any future policies and practices.

Section III: Technology

In this section of the literature review, I will look closely at technology and why and how they are used in the classroom. It is generally acknowledged that in education a continuous frequent task is for educators to arrange, convey and revise instruction intended to assist students in achieving curriculum goals. When we verbalize about technology, we have a tendency to refer to computers, as an effective tool for addressing such goals. Computers have had an enormous impact on the art education world. They have given art educators a new set of virtual tools for creating and making art (Ragins, 2007).

Therefore, it would reckless of me not to mention and discuss computers in the classroom. Some art educators jump at the chance to use this new technology, which have only practical applications to the field of art not the teaching art based education. It also takes away of my belief that art educators should focus on art based education integration. The primary function of this new technology is to process image creations for art students.

The story of educational technology perspective. What will follow is an attempt to reveal how art educators are influenced by technology and examine some practices of computers uses in the art classroom. Technology is a catalyst for changes in classroom processes because it provides a distinctive departure, revolutionized in context that advocates alternative ways of operation (Sandholtz, Ringstaff and Dwyer, 1997). Stallard and Cocker (2001) wrote that in the early adoption and use of the microcomputer were similar to the adoption used by other technologies when first introduced. One example was the motion picture camera, its fixed position aimed at the theater stage recording the action of actors so an audience would experience it. Innovators moved the camera out from inside the theater to outside venues; hence the field of cinematography was created.

The microcomputer first made its appearance in K-12 schools in the late 1970's, with the Commodore Pet, TRS-80 Model and the Apple computer leading the way.

As with the motion picture camera, whose first use replicated an obvious, existing application, the idea that the computer would make an effective "teacher" or teaching machine reflected the same mind-set: "use new technology to accomplish old tasks" (Stallard & Cocker, 2001).

By the 1980s, computers had established footholds in schools. The educational market, the computer and software industries developed comprehensive packages that covered an entire course of study. This was called integrated learning systems or ILS. The management portion of the ILS was attractive to teachers and administrators and the software companies centered around integrated learning systems. Eventually, IBM PC's entered into the market, with Apple computers dominating the K-12 market from the 1980s and mid 1990s but, then losing that lead to Wintel platform (an acronym for Windows and Intel). The driving force behind K-12 education was computer integration (Stallard & Cocker, 2001).

By the early 1990s, the arrival of computer networking combined with open standards for electronic communications ignited the greatest gains for productivity in our history. IBM created its Token Ring technology that quickly conquered the market for data communications. If you purchased IBM equipment, you had to be connected to peripherals made by IBM and install and use software supported by IBM.

Ethernet, a protocol for transferring data over wires of fibers, became the industry standard and replaced IBM's Token Ring and all other networking systems. This drove prices down so school districts could meet the expense of installing local wide area networks, which was a synchronous communication (sending and receiving information concurrent in time). With the application of the Internet, an Asynchronous communication (those not concurrent in time) replaced the Ethernet.

Banking institutions have adopted this type of technology as a universal operation, across the nation and worldwide. The installation and implementation of an, Asynchronous Transfer Mode, directs their customers with banking solutions in the form of questions. Sample questions, "If you know your account, please enter it now"? If you type the correct response, a list of options will appear which are controlled by a small numbered keyboard. Options include withdrawal, deposit, and transfer, balance inquiry for savings and checking, to name a few. The following transactions are understood and practiced by all, without hesitations or equivocations. Everyone is encouraged to achieve success within the banking institutions; failure subsequently is unacceptable, for the reason that mastering these techniques will facilitate you securing funds. Most people are acquainted with this particular electronic wizardry as an ATM, which an acronym for Automatic Teller Machine.

By the mid-1990s to early 2001, information became stored on bulletin boards, then later on the Internet. It was realized as an innovative and effective teaching and learning resource beyond the computer. Distance learning provided access with human experts in collaboration with students and teachers. Students and teachers were able to submitted inquiries to question or problems to those experts through asynchronous responds using e-mail or bulletin boards. These also shift the educational format adventuring outside the classroom to the world. (Stallard and Cocker, 2001).

In mid 2001 to mid 2003, satellite-based distance learning systems have been introduced into the K-12 education. This technology allows broadcast-quality video and very expensive broadband networking in support for learning that is synchronous (teacher and students together, at the same time but at different places, each viewing and speaking to each other). There are virtual schools in Canada, Florida, just to name a few, are beginning to experiment with this new technology called "classroom without walls". However, before looking towards future technology, there are still elements for the K-12 educational environment that must be considered before any further electronic resources can be placed into perspective (Stallard & Cocker, 2001).

Technology in the classroom. As stated in previous sections, many art educators at the national levels adapt and adjust to different current practices of teaching art education within their classroom. With computers there is a wide range of acceptance and uses in the classroom. Greh (1990) writes, "There are, however, a great number of art educators who are anxious to try computers in their classroom, but are not quite sure what computers can do, and how they might be used within the art curriculum" (p. 125). Greh also suggests some answers to the purpose of computers, she writes:

> What computers may do are present artist, art teacher, and students' artist with the possibility of expanding artistic vision, of watching ideas grow, and of playing with and integrating images. Computers provide many students with a non-threatening environment in which to play with images . . . risk free (p.125).

With this kind of approach, this would alter the way art based education is being taught by teachers, and students' definition and focus of art education will be fun and games, not knowledge, concepts or skills.

Gigliotti (1998) examines the conflicting theories and practices that contemporary educators encounter involving art projects and computer technologies. Gigliotti realizes a strong resistance of the art world for emerging aesthetic of interactivity, calling for an involvement for the development of computer technology between artist and art educators.

That resistance can be attributed to the fact that the art educational world failure to endorse one universal practice for the delivery of instructions for teaching art based education from teacher to teacher. With this kind of approach it's difficult to establish a distinction between certified teachers and teacher artist and an artist.

Promley and Stewart (1997) discuss how the involvement of art teachers assist the students' learning with digital images increased students' engagement in learning art history's discipline and research. The art teachers' input was crucial for the development of technological software. Clearly, this is a step in the right direction, but the focus should be how to create practical classroom applications for technology. Too much time would be wasted on technology and its development, not art education, which prove less beneficial to students with continued resistance for adoption by teachers. Gerrish (2000) writes, "I sensed a talented group of artists and teachers with an extraordinarily complex set of skills would lose relevance because they would resist using one more tool . . . technology" (p. 34-39). About students learning with computers, Gerrish writes:

> One of the things I noticed was the frequency in which students made similar errors on the computer and at the art table. If a student had difficulty with symmetry or mirrored spatial relationships in the real-world model, it was a given that they would have the same difficulty in their virtual model. One might think that a student's experience in solving a problem in one arena would eliminate the same problem in the other arena, but this is not the case (p. 34-39).

Finally, the question of the use of technology in art based education, especially since art based education classrooms have always had implications for hands-on education, is likely to be a matter of that art education teacher's own belief and practice. This examination seeks some answers about the effective use of computers, in the art based education classroom, as an integral part of major art based education implementations.

Summary. Unlike discipline based art education and current practices, technological reforms in art education is a more realistic necessity than theoretical art education integration. Computers have progressively moved to gain the awareness among art teachers, with some uncertainties, as a tool for learning. Some art teachers quickly distinguish their responsibility helping students think comprehensively about the new medium. The literature traces the history of computers in the classroom and the evolution of its role of innovations for students learning applications. The literature suggests that art education has an enormous advantage in the use of technological paradigms over the other subject areas. Briefly, these changes to art education by technology reveal that technology is a new medium of expression and communication, which is not less important to the content traditional art education emulates.

Art based education teachers providing instruction in middle schools must understand there are dangers in accepting the computer, as part of their lesson plans or art program. Unless, a clear purpose in using the computer is implemented and strategies developed. Art teachers acknowledge that technology is revolutionizing the world and how educational communities are learning how they can be use effectively in the classroom. The art based education teacher should utilize and learn the best features of the computer graphic programs for furthering and understand the art for the students.

The computer should not determine the content of how art should be taught. Focusing on technology for just playing as you learn will result in limiting the effects of critical thinking. Technology requires critical understanding of the tool and of the expectations of their students. With new software such as Microsoft Publisher, Power Point, Computer Aided Design (CAD) just to name a few, an art based teacher doesn't teach art or art education, they teach the computer software. These practices reduced the role of art based education and its relationship within the educational community as a core subject.

Inclusive summary. Concluding observations about DBAE, current practices and computers, this study looks at art educators' knowledge, interpretation and implementation of the latest art education reform initiatives, in urban middles school, with special attention to discipline-based art education, current practices and technology.

Art education teachers, whether they are intentionally aware of it, are teaching how they have been taught throughout their teaching career. And for good reason, the concept of their work is fashioned through manipulation of the school environment and experiences of imaginative self-expression that molded their creative expression, their conceptions art and knowledge in art (Lowenfeld and Brittain, 1984). This creative paradigm, of self-expression, dominated art education for years. The need to increase art integration continues and has significant persuasion in art based education.

During the Getty Center for Art Education, the center became tantamount with discipline-based art education (DBEA) (Dobbs, 1998). The Center advocated and supported the DBAE approach, the Center set the original definition for the practices of how DBEA is taught. The problem, however, is that The Center did not adopt or include one urban school education approach, leaving the choice to individual persons or group values. DBEA has roots of enduring racism and their disciplines are applicable to certain groups (Fehr, Fehe & Keifer-Boyd, 2000). Additionally, such programs try including some multicultural contents to address ethic and racial diversity in the classroom, but it failure for inclusion of urban middle school students diminishes the distinguishing quality of art education.

Today, some art education curricula have expanded to address the issue of Teaching Artist. Teaching Artist was the cure-all holistic approach for urban schools, charged with teaching a view of aesthetic experiences of the arts (Burrows, and Waldorf, 2003). The literature does not report any comprehensive art based education program for urban middle school students that stimulate a creative capacity and scholarly approaches to this issue. While different comprehensive art programs being adopted by schools in this nation, so are classroom practices. With the institution of street corner versions, of DBAE, there emerge several concerns for what art teachers are doing and teaching in their classroom. The opportunity to engage in real life integration, within the core subject areas, those concerns are compounded with the vulnerability of teacher's concepts, understanding and implementation of theories involving classroom practices. In other words, if a common language, practice and policies are not adopted by all art educational groups; there will continuous non effective art versions for teaching art based education.

Part of the curriculum development in art education is to necessitate the use of technology, computers, in the art education classroom. Technology offers art education a guarantee of an innovative rich form of expression. Greh (1990) believes that teachers operating in isolation throughout the country and without the validity of curriculum development based on experiences, will fall short attempting in developing a foundation based on principles of art education. Technology alone will not present its benefits except by the reliability of the teacher. Unfortunately, the system is malfunctioning when many of the content selection include integration for the core subject areas, in regards to technology.

What I am trying to say is that most educational institutions use technology to further dissolve the name art education, creating a different kind of curriculum and provide workshops for teachers to learn these innovative concepts in order to teach the students, the most recent paradigm, Digital Storytelling. A workshop was designed to acquaint teachers with the discovery of how students can use digital tools to find and showcase their personal voice. That digital storytelling weaves voice and multimedia together to transform the personal narrative through images, narration, and background music. They learn to apply the seven elements of digital storytelling as way to review and evaluate digital stories.

Teachers learn to implement steps for planning, crafting and producing a digital story and technologies that support the process. Implementations in the classroom and digital stories for other genre are briefly being discussed. They influence teachers that digital storytelling is fun, is a way for students to better express themselves, and meets Grade Level Content Expectations.

It is my belief that this approach takes the place of hands on experiences those students gets when mixing media, instead of pushing a button. The environment of the art education classroom transformed from the development of skills and concepts to digital arrangements and applications on a screen. Projects that were once produced on drawing paper are now produced on copier printing paper. The finding of the literature indicates that:

1) DBAE or a comprehensive advancements learning about art suggests some centralization for art reforms.

2) DBAE advocates consider that DBAE is, and continues to be, the most momentous influence on art education theory and practice.

3) Ambiguity exists in the teacher's knowledge, interpretation, and implementation of technology and theories of DBAE. With the DBAE programs aimed at cultural pluralism, even in scholarly literature, the efforts to implement of inclusion have affected urban middle school students negatively.

Chapter V

CLASSROOM PRACTICES

As an Art Education teacher for many years, I've discovered that there are several organizations, such as the Getty Foundation, The Getty Center, the National Art Education Association just to name a few, that dictate why and how art education should be taught across the nation. For urban school students these organizations fail to address the importance of how art based education can enhance the educational process using the four core subject areas (mathematics, science, social studies, and language arts). Most of these groups and organizations advocate discipline-based art education (DBAE), which were discussed in detail in chapter four. It is my contention that the four core subject areas should be integrated into art based education curriculum lessons. With the achievement gap between urban and rural schools, increasing, over the last decade, urban schools need to find new strategies for tackling this problem.

Researching this problem, I have found that there was a lot of information about achievement gaps, so I made the decision to focus on and report on sciences. Using the Oak Park Schools MEAP (Michigan Education Assessment Program) I compared the scores to the NAEP (National Assessment Education Progress) for science achievement-level results by race / ethnicity for 8th grade. The actual patterns of achievement had a major statistically significant difference from 1996-2001 in students' average scores national. Oak Park's proficient percentage was much higher, during that time period, from 6.8% to 18.6%, but since then it has fallen below the national average for urban schools. With the federal No Child Left Behind and Michigan's Education Yes legislation being aggressively enforced, more urban schools are forced to improve their test score. Also, more schools are asked to perform at higher academic standards each year with threats of hostile takeover by charter schools if they fail.

Currently, in the Oak Park School District, the African-American students tend to regard art based education as frivolous classes where learning stops and playtime begins! I believe that my innovative lesson plans and contributions to educational community will help elevate the position regarding teaching art based education and its applications for cross curricular learning. This would clearly justify and make a good argument for classifying art education as a subject area. Manner (2002) writes:

> Curriculum integration is not a new idea, but it bears reexamination in schools today, where standards-driven academic concerns may require educators to look at school subjects in isolation rather than in ways that enhance perceptions of their connections.

Lemlech (1998) described integration as the attempt to "link subject fields and learning processes" rather than focusing on a single subject discipline (p. 170). As Wishon, Crabtree, and Jones (1998) recommended, teachers who wish to integrate curriculum should "frequently" ask themselves which content and process objective from the various discipline overlap, are related, and can be taught simultaneously. As beneficial as curriculum integration can be, however, Posner and Rudnitsky (2001) have noted that integration and single discipline-based activities in the classroom both have their place in a balanced program.

Now, let's look at some examples of lesson plans for the 6th, 7th, and 8th grades I have created and that were successful for art education integration.

6th Grade Lesson Plan

Defining Art and Art Education. Before students can understand, comprehend and apply the strategies of art based education integration, the difference between Art and Art education must be defined. So, I begin with my sixth grade classes discussing the difference between Art and Art Education with visual references. These visual references are pictures that I have drawn for the purpose of this discussion for establishing the two definitions. It's important that I tell the students that any examples of works of art shown, presented or used as an example, I am the artist and will never use other artist's works of art. Using other student's artwork from examples from my initial instructions will be used as a tool to show how other students resolved the problems.

The reason for this decision is simple and I explain it to students with this approach. If you walked into a math class and saw the teacher writing math problems on the board, that teacher could explain principles and procedures how to solve the problems. The same goes for science, social studies or any subject areas that teacher should display the skills necessary to teach you. By using my works of art it confirms my command of the subject area and how art education will be taught.

The lesson. Before showing the students the first of three visual references, I asked them a question; "What do you see?" The first picture is a colored pencil drawing of the Incredible Hulk and the Silver Surfer on his surfboard (see Figure 1). The students' responses were similar. Some said that they saw a picture of two cartoon characters. Only a few knew the proper names of the two characters, but that was expected. After listening to those who wanted to answer the question I made the statement, "Now let tell you what you don't see!" Confirming the names of the two characters, I proceeded to point out that there were no trees, birds, sky, mountains, ground or any objects that would give the viewer indications of where the two characters are located—that the Incredible Hulk, who is looking up into the air as his hand is reaching for something that has caught his attention and the Silver Surfer is using his arm power to obliterate a metal cylinder before flying away on his surfboard. Both characters are moving in opposite directions. With both characters looking and going in opposite directions, it is safe to say that both characters do not even acknowledge the existence of each other.

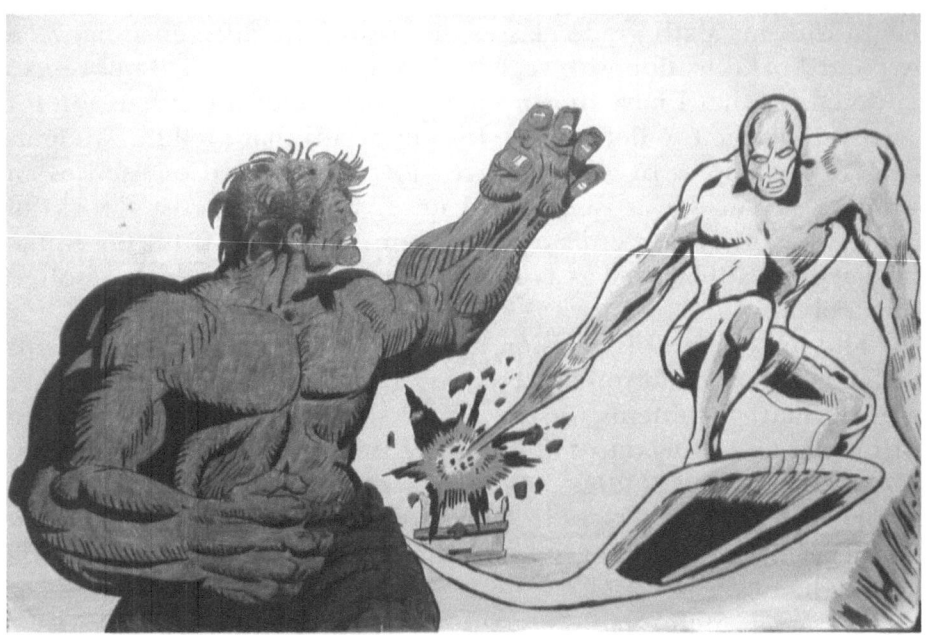

Figure 1. Incredible Hulk

The next question I asked was if I took the picture of the Incredible Hulk out of the drawing, would it change the picture? Then I asked the same question with the Silver Surfer, then with both characters out of the drawing. The answer was background or visual references tying the cartoon characters together, the removal of them both would not change the drawing. That was an introduction of the visual references I want the students looking for in the next two drawings.

The next drawing was a picture of two more cartoon characters drawn with colored pencils (see Figure 2). Thor the Thunder God is standing on a rock with his hammer raved back, his arm stretched and he is looking upward bracing himself for another attack. There was a falling solider with his head in hands, lying at Thor's feet. There were lines that divided the picture, a headings and a text box. Again, I asked the question, "What you see?" I found a very small number of students knew the main characters proper name (Thor). Based on the information and strategies given on the first picture more students participated in the discussion. After listening to the students' responses, I made the statement, "Now, let me tell you what you don't see!"

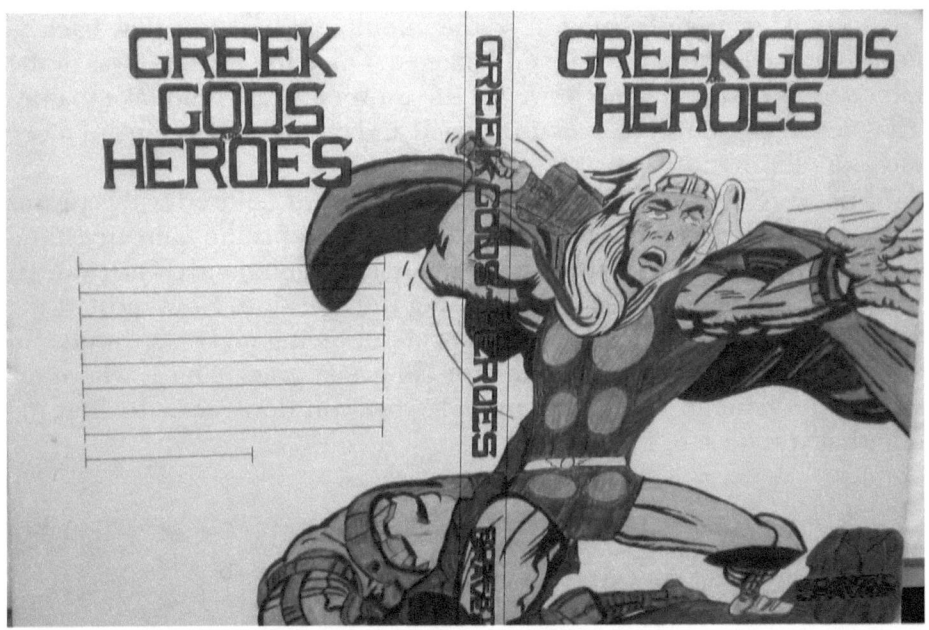

Figure 2. Thor the Thunder God

What you don't see is that the picture was unsuccessful at giving any indicators or clues of where this conflict is taking place. With the white sky in the background this tells us that the location of this battle takes place on another planet and solar system. Of all of the planets in our solar system we don't have planets with white skies. You don't see why this character, Thor the Thunder God, is bracing for another attack. Let me set the stage and tell the story about Thor. Thor the Thunder God is the son of Odin, the King of the Greek Gods and not to be confused with the King of the Roman Gods Zeus. In case you don't know the Greeks and Roman had different names for the same Gods that perform the same tasks. If Odin should become ill or die, Thor is heir to throne. Thor has an evil half brother, named is Loki. Loki tried to convince Odin that he should be the rightful heir to the throne without success. Since that day, Loki has been trying to create ways to kill Thor. Loki has amassed several huge armies in an attempt to kill Thor that failed. The last attempt Loki made against Thor was the attack of the 100 foot giant stone behemoth. This behemoth was made of grayish stone holding a metal spiked club. Since Thor controls the elements, like the wind, rain, lighting and thunder with his hammer, he summoned all those powers to unite. Thor threw the hammer at the giant creature and upon contact the behemoth exploded into millions of small pebbles destroying the creature. After the destruction of the enemy the hammer flew back to its owner like a guided missile undamaged. Once the hammer was in the hands of Thor, there is no power in the universe that could take it away. That day, again, Loki escaped unharmed and continued to think of more ways for eliminating Thor.

The third drawing (see Figure 3) is of a deer colored with crayons standing in tall green grass. After asking the students the same question, "Want do you see?" the entire class began raising their hands. They wanted to engage in the discussion of answering the question. Now, most of the students' responses began with talking about seeing no background and a deer in the foreground standing in tall green grass. This is where my statement changed from, "Let me tell what you don't see," to "Let me tell what you do see."!

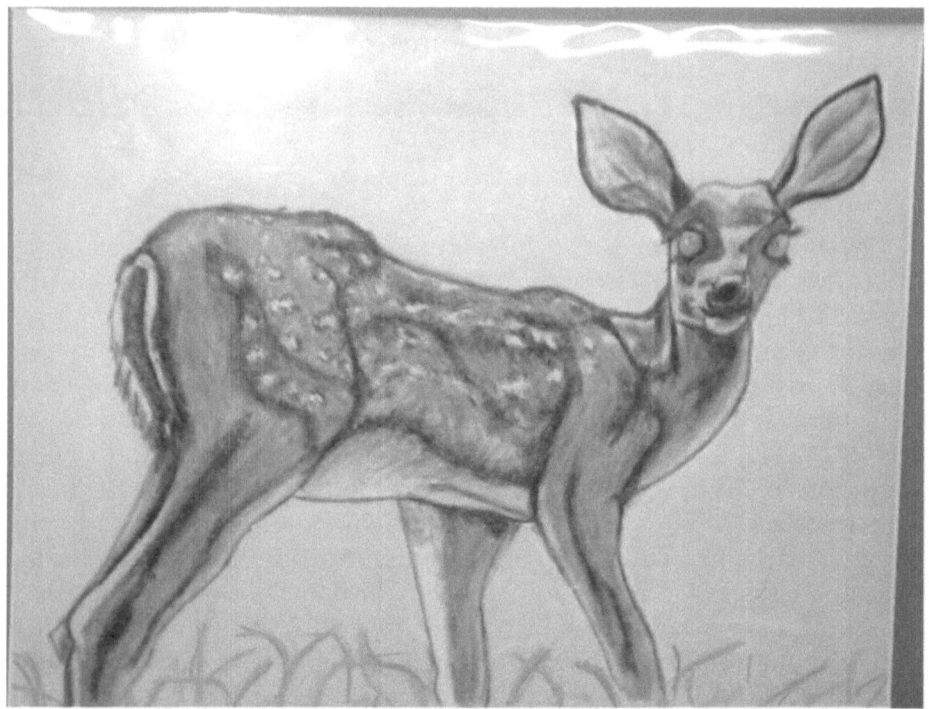

Figure 3. Deer Standing in Tall Green Grass

What you see here in this picture is a deer standing in tall green grass. Scientists have discovered only one planet in our solar system which has grass. What is that planet? The students' responses were the same, Earth! I said, that's right! I continued, what you also see are that the background with the deer and the grass all are members of the same color family called earth tones. Now, what you think you see is the absence of black. Then I asked the question, How many of you think you see (even though black is not a color, I am using it to prove a point) the color black? The students responded by saying, the deer's nose is black and the outlining of the deer. I say to them, "This is what I'm going to do. I am going to bring the drawing to each table, and then very closely look at the nose and the outline of the deer. Please, don't say or yell out loud your discovery until everyone has viewed the drawing!" As the picture traveled from table to table, the eyes of the students were opening wide in astonishment. Like a deer whose eyes were captured by headlights of a car crossing the road at night, the students were frozen in suspended animation. Now, asking the student again, "was the deer's nose and the outline of the deer black?" They all answered no! I began explaining the illusion by saying, "The nose of the deer and the outline of the deer appeared to be black because you have to know and understand how to mix and match colors. Knowing that when you put a certain dark colors next to certain light colors an illusion occurs. The dark color will absorb the light and the light colors will reflect the light. That's why the purple nose and outline of the deer appeared to look as though it's black.

Putting down the picture of the deer, I picked up the first drawing saying, now, here is the first picture. Looking at the Incredible Hulk you primarily see three colors, olive green for his skin, royal purple for his pants and he is outlined in the actual color black. The Silver Surfer and his surfboard are shades of light blue showing the dark areas and light silver. There is a store very close where you can purchase every super hero that has been created. You can trace them, color them as they appear, change their colors or do anything you want with them.

Holding the first picture in one hand, the picture of the deer in the other hand and say, now, look at the picture of the deer again. As you can see it takes more knowledge, skills and understanding in order to draw the picture of the deer than the first picture. Science is integrated into the creation of this picture, because mixing of colors has to do with chemistry and the deer is a part of life science. So, with that in mind, the first drawing would be considered Art! The third drawing would be considered as Art Based Education! Now, let's define the terms Art and Art Based Education. Art is a craft and Art Based Education is a step-by-step process through demonstrations with integration across the curriculum you learn. In this class you will learn and apply Art Based Educational concepts and skills. Now if anyone should ask you what the difference between Art and Art Based Education is, you will be able to tell them. Now, does anyone have any questions?

In each class the students were amazed and expressed how little they actually knew about art and art based education. The students could not believe how they had learned so much just from such a simple lesson. They expressed gratitude and wanted to get started immediately on how they could learn more and start utilizing new concepts and skills. Overall, the students were most interested in the art based education integration and asked if other schools adopted this concept of teaching art in this manner. I told them that I was creator of this Art Based Education integration concept and that they were the only students who are experiencing this method at present.

Gunzenhauser and Gerstl-Pepin (2002) discuss how the North Carolina A+ Schools Program initiated an arts-integration pilot phases in 25 schools when the state increased the stakes of standardized testing. They report:

> The A+ Program was based loosely on Gardner's 1983 Theory of Multiple Intelligence. The theory was central to the program in the belief that the ability of the arts and curriculum program exposed teachers to the theory of multiple intelligences and methods of two-way arts integration (arts integration into the standard curriculum and the standard curriculum integrated into the arts) (p. 3-14).

It would be interesting to revisit this school system five years from now and evaluate its integration plan. I am curious to know, if in fact, integration of art education has made a difference in increasing standardized test scores in the state.

7th Grade Lesson

Two point perspective and soft pastels. First, I began the lesson by reviewing the two definitions of the word perspective. Remember there are two definitions of the word perspective. Let's review the first. Do you recall a story or whether you saw a fight in the cafeteria and the person investigating the fight wanted to know you're what? The student responded by saying "opinion", and I would say, that's right! The other definition is where you are when you are viewing an object. Remember when I had a student stand next to me who was shorter than me? Do you remember that I said that the two of us were different in height and we both had different views of an object? That view is called perspective, so lets get started. We are going to construct five boxes in two-point perspective with different views.

First, I began by telling the students to fold their drawing paper in half evenly the long way. Using newsprint paper (18"x 12") I asked the students to open the paper, take their ruler, place it underneath the crease and draw a light construction line with a number two pencil. "Remember, this line is called the eye level line." At the ends of the eye level line, on both sides of the paper, I asked the students to put a small dark dot.

Remember these dark dots are called vanishing points. Remember that a vanishing point is where all the lines converge in a perspective drawing. Since this is a review; I'm going to review this as though you are hearing for the first.

So, if there any new students you'll be up to the same level as the other students. Now, somewhere in the middle of the paper, on the eye level line, with a ruler draws a two inch line vertically. Do you recall that the eye level line always cut the object in half? So, the length of the vertical line is one above and below the eye level line. With your ruler, converge the top and bottom of that vertical line in the center to both vanishing points. Make sure you check with the schematic on the board at anytime to confirm your progress. Your drawing and the schematic must look the same before you continue.

On the two lines on the top and bottom, converging to the vanishing points, you measure the width and length of the box. Remember to always start your measuring from the center vertical line, and then make your marks. With your ruler, connect the markings from the top and bottom lines; this will form the sides of the box. The center vertical line and the lines on both sides of the box should be parallel. Parallel lines are lines that run in the same direction.

Using a box that was placed on top of the cabinet next to the chalkboard, I said, "Looking at this box above, you can see the front vertical line, the two sides or the edges of the box. You can not see the opposite side of box, but we know its there. The way we will show the opposite side of the box is with hidden lines. Hidden lines are illustrated by using short dash lines from the top and bottom of both lines on the side of the box to the vanishing points. After drawing these examples on the board, I said, Now, see where the two hidden lines have crossed, in the middle of the box, the two lines form the letter x. Place your rules at the center of each x and draw a hidden line that will connect them. Now, you can see the both sides of the box, the inside hidden part and the top of the box. This was the completion of box number one. The vertical line for box number two starts at the bottom of the paper. Not close to the bottom, not in the vicinity or in the area, but at the bottom of the paper!

Repeating steps one-three, from the schematic, I stopped and asked the students this question:

> What kind of view is this? The students responded, "bird's eye view!" I said, That's right! Now, when you measure in this view you must measure on the two top lines from the center vertical line. Then use your ruler and draw a line straight down, on both sides, to next box line. If you measure on the top line lines box proportions will be incorrect! Make sure the center vertical and the two lines on the sides are parallel. Adding the hidden lines to box number three made it complete.

At this point, I drew two vertical lines, one evenly between boxes three and one and this was the beginning of box number four. The other vertical line was drawn and placed evenly between boxes one and two and this was the beginning of box number five. Now, you construct box number four just like you constructed box number three. You construct box number five just like you construct box number two. Here are your measurements for each box and you can see that each box has different measurements. Remember you must reverse the mathematical equation L x W x H (length times width times height)! The H is the center vertical line and I underlined all of those measurements with yellow chalk. The W is the right parallel line and the L is the left parallel line. Make sure you construct the boxes in sequential order as they appear on the board.

Introduction of soft pastels. Once the boxes were completed I introduced the application of soft pastels. When you have completed all of the boxes, I want you to erase the vanishing points, the construction lines(the lines that converge to the vanishing points) and the hidden lines. I just want to see your boxes only! Of course some of the students were upset that they had to erase all of those lines, so I reminded them this was a review! They had to transfer their completed boxes onto a white drawing paper using an ebony pencil. With an ebony pencil, what you do is turn the paper on the back, darken the boxes with the ebony pencil, place it on the white drawing paper, with tape in the corners so it will not move, then trace over the boxes with a drawing pencil.

The ebony pencil acted like carbon paper, so everything that had been touched by the ebony pencil and outlined transferred. Taping several boxes, in two-point perspective a white drawing paper drawing, on the board I began giving instruction on how to use soft pastel. I said, this is a soft pastel. It's similar to chalk but the ingredients to make pastels are different. It has a softer quality when you apply it on paper. You'll see as I demonstrate how to use it! First, let's establish from what direction our light source is coming from, it will determine what colors that will be used. We will use yellow colored pastels on the light side of the box. A green colored pastel on the opposite side of the box. And a spring green colored pastel, which is a light green, for the transition color.

Covering the box with a small amount of pastel, I said, when you apply the pastel use a small amount, take your finger and rub the pastel into the area you want covered. As the pastels began blending into the box, the students were amazed at the results. Just remember, there are several important rules! Don't put a lot of pastels on the paper, don't blow any residue in the air or on the floor, make sure your fingers are clean and last don't get it all over yourself!

This assignment was enjoyed by all the students and the only complaint was getting messy fingers!

8th Grade Lesson

A children's storybook. While attending numerous art educational workshops, during some of my summer months, the focus at those workshops was discipline-based art education (DBAE) driven. My search for new innovative ideas to improve my eight grade lessons, A Children's Storybook, created lots of frustration and disillusionment. The storybooks the students were producing were artistically wonderful but their creative writing and editing skills were poor. To make this lesson complete, I thought, my skills in language arts and my writing abilities would have to improve in order for my students to be successful. My search to resolve this issue led me to enroll in the Oakland Writing Project Summer Institute 2000. In partnership with The University of Michigan, Adrian College and Oakland Schools Intermediate School District (ISD), this institute was a month long intensive Writing-to-Read and Reading-to-Write. The instructors for the institute consisted of two professors, one from Adrian College, one from the University of Michigan; they were a husband and wife team. The other instructor was a retired Language Arts teacher. She had taught in Michigan's Walled Lake School District for thirty-five years.

The workshop. Enrolled in the workshop were twenty-five language arts teachers and of course, I was the only art based education teacher. In the first session, my excitement level was extremely high and my desire to uncover the missing element for my children's storybook lesson had begun! We sat at long light gray rectangular tables arraigned in a U-shaped that sat all twenty-five of us comfortably.

The instructors began by introducing themselves, and then asked each participant to follow. As part of introduction, we had to include our subject and reasons for attending the workshop. The room filled out with cries for reform, more directions and ideas for the improvement of their students' writing skills. Finally, it was my turn to speak. Proud of my subject area and my conviction, I introduced myself with pride along with the reason for attending the workshop. My expressed concerns poured like the opening of the floodgates of a dam. On that day, the cold artic gale winds of November came early shown by the frozen cold-blue faces of the other teachers. There was dead silence in the room! The instructors were amazed and caught off guard but were not bothered by this sudden intrusion from an outsider. At first, I was not accepted as a peer because of my subject area but later that would change.

The workshop format. After concluding the formal introductions of all the participants the instructors discussed the format for the workshop, which was the following:

I. Parts of Reading Workshop
    a. Mini-Teams
    b. Reading Times
    c. Sharing

II. Tools
    a. Reading Logs
    b. Response Journals
    c. Book Shares d. Projects

III. Types of Reading Experiences
    a. Whole group reading (guided reading / paired reading)
    b. Small group reading (Literature Circle)
    c. Individual Choice Reading

Presentation/Demonstration Guidelines. Begin with a question about your teaching practices

- Past Practice: What you did? What worked out and what didn't? How would you modify according to what you have learned? If possible, include student work samples.
- Problem Solving Question or next steps for you as a teacher: Develop and plan new teacher practice using key workshop principles and focusing on a practical solution for your classroom.

- Inquiry Issue or Question that came with or that has emerged for you. What did you learn? What are methods, ideas and activities that are applicable in the classroom?

Confirmation. Everyday a fifteen to twenty minute writing topic was assigned to the groups. The topics varied from personal to classroom experiences. We shared our writing assignments by reading them aloud to the class. My topics focus mostly about my childhood and my relationship with my father. Writing about those experiences was easy and I could express myself though words. By the end of the second week, the majority of the group and even the instructors anxiously awaited my topic. By the end of the third week, I had been accepted as true language arts practitioner. My acceptance into the group was confirmed and validated by a quote in the textbook introduced the week of that class. The book was The Art of Teaching Writing, New Edition, in which Calkins (1994) writes:

> If our teaching is to be art, we must draw from all we know, feel and believe in order to create something beautiful. To teach well, we do not need more techniques and strategies as much as we need vision of what is essential. It is not the number of good ideas that turns our work into art but the selection, balance and design of those ideas. Artist knows this. Artistry does not come from the quantity of red and yellow paint or from the amount of clay or marble but from the organizing *vision* that shapes the use of these materials. It comes from a sense of priority and design (p. 3).

After the instructor read that quote, all eyes had turned, looked at me and I was given the biggest smile of acceptance.

Creation of the children's storybook. As a final project, we were asked to take one of our current lesson plans and revised it using techniques learned in the workshop. My body temperature began to heat up and glow, like the underbody of the space shuttle's re-entry into the earth atmosphere; I chose my eighth grade Children's Storybook lesson. Using the techniques learned, the lesson had to be broken into three individual parts and make the length of the book ten pages. This was essential in order to get the most effective productivity from the students. Each part has its own directions and instructions as follows:

Illustration

Artist:
1. Cover—Draw where the story takes place.
2. Introduction—Draw the character(s).
3. Who—Draw the character(s) in a setting?
4. Who—Draw a one-point perspective object(s)?
5. What—Draw what the character(s) is doing?
6. What—Page 6 and Why—7 are continuous pages, place the
7. The character(s) in a setting.
8. Why—Draw a two-point perspective object(s).
9. Whom-Draw who the character(s) are talking to (audience).
10. Effect-Draw how the character(s) were affected by the story.

Storyline

Author:

1. Cover—Write the title and subtitle.
2. Introduction—Write to introduce the character(s).
3. Who—Write about the character(s)
4. Who—Continue to write about the character(s)
5. What—Write about the activities of the character(s)
6. What—Continue to write about the activities of the character(s)?
7. Why—Write to explain the character(s) action or purpose.
8. Why—Continue to write about the character(s) action or purpose.
9. Whom—Write about the audience (who is being talked to).
10. Effect—Write a conclusion (persuades or expresses a lesson to be learned).

Publication

Editor:

1. Check for the title and subtitle.
2. Make sure that all the character(s) are colored / complete.
3. Make sure that the storyline is complete.
4. Check the number of pages (10).
5. Make sure the words match the pictures.

6. Get personal information about each group member (Names / their part in the book / future college / a brief statement about the book).
7. Put pictures and story together in book form.
8. Conference with teacher (10-15 minutes).
9. Reread and double-check pictures and story.
10. Glue / paste words and pictures together just the way you want it.
11. CONGRATULATIONS! YOU'RE PUBLISHED!

Making transparences of this revised lesson plan along with my previous lesson plan my presentation was ready. Using an overhead projector the instructors and the participants were amazed. This was the most productive summer and most rewarding.

This workshop solidified my ideas the efforts to integrate art based education in language arts and cross curriculum learning is possible. Wilson, (1998) writes:

> I believe that curriculum integration is not only the wave of the future in education, it will become the prescribed method of teaching nationwide as we move into the 21st century (p. 34-5). Manner (2002) sums it best as she writes: Art integration requires daily acknowledgement of the ways in which art is an essential form of human communication and expression. When we do this, art's place within the "core curriculum" as an embedded tool becomes apparent. Art education should not be seen as a separate compartment, but as an integral part of the educational process (p. 17-19).

Summary. These events have fashioned my artistic career and my life. The experiences have determined the conduit for my teaching style of Art Based Education and have inspired innovative processes for current practices and theories for integrating the four disciplines into lesson plans. Such a style of teaching (art education curricula) and the challenge of integrating four core subject areas, innovative ideas and instructional approaches, suggest that personal theories and practices involved in the educational process in, urban school middle school setting, art education curricula might be understood.

There are organizations that continue to exclude urban schools during the conception or development for reforms of art based educational theories and practices. As a result, they marginalize the artist lives and experiences of urban teachers such as me, and they fail to address the academic needs of my students. School districts across the nation adopted those art education reforms and receive grants and funds from that organization. Unfortunately, the focus is on content issues that are highly specialized and not on ways to integrate art based education into the educational process.

MacPherson (2004) reports in *The Detroit News* that The No Child Left Behind Law that Art, which is routinely viewed as an electives and is not tested, is especially vulnerable to being diminished or even cut entirely. MacPherson writes:

> Under the NCLB, arts education was listed as a core subject for the first time in federal education law. But reports released over the past several months have documented that art classes are getting squeezed out of the schools because the federal law doesn't require that students be tested for their proficiency in art, music, dance or drama (p. 9a).

Summary.

With this study I'm trying to persuade the national art organizations, The National Art Education Association, The Getty Foundation, The Getty Center, just to name a few, to re-examine its advocacy of DBAE being the best practices and re-evaluate those organizations, the National Art Counsel, National Art Education Educators, just to name a few, that have been awarded financial assistance to perpetuate their beliefs. These awards have been in the form of grants, scholarships and teachers salaries. If these national art organizations began to understand they need to become revolutionary leaders to initiate reforms through, transformational and transactional leadership, it may help other educators and parents re-evaluate their method and attitudes towards the dissemination of art instruction.

Ultimately, I suggest that a ground-breaking procedure, by the national art educational organizations, of the examination of any attempts to endorse art based education integration application is pivotal for the improvement in art educational policies, practices and the establishment of a common objective. Once this common objective is acknowledged, this kind of development ought to give encouragement to all art education teachers who need to constantly ask themselves what they are teaching, why they are teaching it, and how can they improve what is being taught, in order to provide a meaningful curriculum.

This study is an attempt to share my vision for improving the ways in which art is experienced by urban school students.

References

Barkan, M. (1955). *A Foundation for Art Education*. New York, NY: Ronald Press

Backer, N. (2001). Art *and Craft education in the U.S. Crafts Report, 28* (5), 22-8; 60-61.

Barnes, R. (2002). *Teaching Art to Young Children 4-9.* (2nd Ed). New York, NY: RoutledgeFalmer, 7-16.

Bereiter, C. (2002). *Education and Mind in the Knowledge Age* Mahwan, NJ Lawrence Erlbaum Associates, Inc., 113-295.

Booth, E. (2003). What is a Teaching Artist? *Teaching Artist Journal, 1,* (1), 45.

Burns, J.M. (1978). *Leadership.* New York, New York: Harper & Row, Publishers, Inc. 200.

Carson, R. (1956). *The sense of wonder.* New York, NY: Harper & Row, Publishers, Inc., 45.

Coleman, F. (1939). Black colleges and the development of an African America visual arts tradition. *International Review of African American Art, 11,* (3), 31-38.

Collins, D. (2001). Educating for interaction. *New Art Examiner, 28* (5), 19-21.

Cornbleth, C. (2000). *Curriculum Politics, Policy Practice: Cases in Corporative Context,* Albany, NY: State University of New York Press, 234.

Cropley, A. (2001). Creativity *in education & learning: a guide for teachers and Educators,* Sterling, VA: Stylus Publishing, 99.

Delacruz, E. (1996). The evolution of discipline-based art education. *The Journal of Aesthetic Education, 30,* 67-82.

Dobbs, S. (1988). *Research Readings For Discipline-Based Art Education: A Journey Beyond Creating.* Reston, VA: National Art Education Association, 112-123.

Dowd, D. (2002). Organizing Art Work Now. *Contemporary Impressions, 10* (2), 14-19.

Efland, A. (2002*). Art and Cognition: Integrating the Visual Arts in the Curriculum.* Reston, VA: Teacher College Press, 48-51.

Erickson, L. (2001). *Stirring the Head, Heart and Soul 63-64* (2nd Ed). Thousand Oaks, CA: Corwin Press Inc.

Fehr, D., Fehr K., & Keifer-Boyd, K. (2000). *Real-World Readings in Art Education: Things Your Professor Never Told You.* New York, NY: Falmer Press, xiii-xvii.

Gardner, H. (1984). *Frames of Mind: Theory of Multiple Intelligences.* New York, NY: Basic Books

Gardner, H. (2004) *The Unschooled Mind: How Children Think and How Schools Should Teach* (10th anniversary Ed). New York, NY: Basic Books

Gerrish, M. (2000). Digital artistry: Technology infused projects created in the Art room. *Multimedia Schools, 7*(5), 34-39.

Getty Institute for Educators on the Visual Arts (1983). *Interim report: Getty Institute for Education on the Visual Arts.* Los Angeles, CA: Getty Center for Education in the Arts.

Getty Center for Education in the Arts. (1985). *Beyond Creating: The Place for Art in America's Schools.* Los Angeles, CA.

Getty, J. Paul. (1998). *Learning in and Through Art: A Guide to Discipline-Based Art* Education.

Gigirotti, C. (1998). Bridge to bridge from: the art, technology and education. *Leonardo 31*(2), 89-92.

Ginsberg, M. & Wlodkowski, R. (2001) *Creating Highly Motivating Classroom of All Students: A school wide Approach to Powerful Teaching with Diverse Learners.* San Francisco, CA: Jossy-Bass.

Goodman, Nelson, (2000). Project Zero: Nelson Goodman's legacy in arts education. *The Journal of Aesthetics and Art Criticism, 58* (3), 245-249.

Gregg, G. (2003). What Are They Teaching Art Students These Days? *Art New, 102* (4), 106-109.

Greh, D. (1990). *Computers in Art Education. Art Education: Secondary Art Education: An Anthology of Issues.* Reston, VA: The National Art Education Association, 125.

Gude, O. & April, A. (1995). What role can art play in education? Olivia Gude and Arnold April: an artist and art educator in dialogue. *New Art Examiner, 22,* 11-13.

Gunzenhauser, M. & Gerstl-Pepin, C. (2002). Guest Editor's Introduction: The Shifting Context of Accountability in North Carolina and Implications for Arts-Based Reform. *Educational Foundations,* 6(2), 3-14.

Hanson, L. (2002). Arts Strengthened in Standards For Teaching Preparation Programs. Sacramento, CA: California Art Education Association, 1-8.

Hoffa, H. (1990). *The Discipline of Art: Secondary Art Education. Secondary Art Education: An Anthology of Issues.* Reston, VA National Art Education Association.

Hoppe, D. (1950). Arts education meets the avant-garde: a postmodern family reunion. *New Art Examiner, 22,* 14-18.

Idaho State Board of Education (2003). *Standards for Visual Arts publication.*

Jarvis, P., Holford, J., & Griffin, C. (1988). The *Theory and Practice of Learning Culture learning.* Sterling, VA: Stylus Publishing, Inc., 66.

Jenkins, P. D. (1986). *A guide for teaching young children.* Englewood Cliffs, NJ: Prentice Hall

Levi, A., & Smith, R. (1991). *Art Education: A Critical Necessity Discipline in Art Education: Content of understanding towards humanities-based conception of DBAE.* Champaign, Ill: University of Illinois Press.

Lowenfeld, V. , Brittain, L. W (1987). *Creative and Mental Growth. 8ᵗʰ Edition* New York, NY: Macmillan. Publishing Co.

MacPherson, K. (2004). No Child Left Behind leaves out art programs: Educators fight to retain classes; as schools focus solely on reading and math. *Detroit News,* 9a.

Manner, J. (2002). Art through the Curriculum. *Kappa Delta Pi Record, 39*(1), 17-19.

Milbrath, C. (1998). Patterns *of artistic development in Children: Comparative Studies of talent.* New York, NY: Cambridge University Press, 29-32

National Board for Professional Teaching Standards: *Early Adolescence Through Young Adulthood Art* (1994).

Nelson, J. (1970). 1 part art + 1 part academics= the Oxbow School. *New Art Examiner,* 28(5), 30-33.

Nestor, J. (1996). Crisis in Prosperity: the art school in America today. *Sculpture* (Washington D.C), 15, 27-9.

North Carolina Public School (2003). *Art Education Curriculum Visual Arts publication* State Board of Education Department of Public Instruction.

Northern Michigan University (2001). Program Summary Art Education; Interstate New Teacher Assessment and Support Consortium (INTASC) Board of Control of Northern Michigan University (Aug. 2001).

Northouse, P. (2001). *Leadership Theory and Practice.* (2nd Ed). Thousand Oaks, CA. Sage Publications, Inc.

Paulson, P. (2003). New Standards for Art Teachers: Perpien Center for Arts Education. *Teaching Artist Journal, 1*(1), 45.

Promey, S. (1953). Digital art history: a new field for collaboration. *American Art, 11,* 36-41.

Riley, R. National standards for arts education part of Goals 2000: Educate American Act, the Clinton Administration's plan for national education reform. *Art & American, 82,* 136.

Rockman, D. (1999). *The Art of teaching Art: A Guide for Teaching and Learning the Foundation of Drawing-Based Art.* New York: Oxford University Press.

Ross, J. (1994). National Standards for Arts Education: The Emperor's New Clothes. *Art Education Policy Review, 96*(2), 26.

Runco, M. (2003). Critical Creative Processes Creeskill, NJ: Hampton Press, Inc. 101

Rusch, A. & Thomas, W. (1990). Are Art Teachers Prepared to Teach The NAEA Essential Components? *Secondary Art Education: An Anthology of Issues.* Reston, VA: The National Art Education Association, 47.

San Jose State University's School of Art (1995). Art Education. *Artweek, 26,* 14-28.

Sandholtz, J. H., Ringstaff, C., & Dwyer, D. (1997). *Teaching with Technology: Creating Student-Center Classroom.* New York, NY: Teachers College Press, 47- 49.

Scehien, F., Steel, T. Expressive education: arts-integrated learning and the role of the artist in transforming the curriculum. Implication of the Erikson Institute Art Projects operating in the public schools of Chicago. *New Art Examiner, 22,* 22-27.

Simpson, J. (1995). Choices for Urban Art Education. *Arts Education Policy Review, 96,* 27-30.

Stallard, C. & Cocker, J. (2001). The *Promise of Technology in Schools: The Net 20 Years.* Lanhan, MD: Rowman & Littlefield Publishers, Inc. 29-37.

Susi, F. (1990). The Art Classroom as a Behavior Setting. *Secondary Art Education: An Anthology of Issues.* Reston, VA The National Art Education Association, 93

The Journal of Aesthetics and Art Criticism, 58, (3) (2000), 245-249.

The National Art Education Association (2002). *Where's Art Now? Support Improving Art Education Polices.*

Tilbury, D. (1994). The critical learning years for environmental education. In R. A. Wilson (Ed.). *Environmental Education at the Early Childhood Level.* Washington, D.C.: North American Association for Environmental Education.

Waldorf, L. (2003). The Making of a Teaching Artist. *Teaching Artist Journal, 1*(1), 13-18.

Watkins, W., Lewis, J., & Chou, V. (2001). Race *and Education: The Roles of History and Society in Education African American Students.* Needham Heights, MA: Allyn & Bacon

Wilson, L. (1998). Life Cycle Flip Books. *Arts & Activities, 124,* 34-35.

Wilson, R. A. (1994). *Environment education at the early childhood level.* Washington, D.C: North American Association for Environment Education.

Zimmerman, E. (1990). Preparing to Teach Art to Secondary Students from All Cultural Backgrounds. *Secondary Art Education: An Anthology of Issues.* Reston, VA The National Art Education Association, 185

www.ingramcontent.com/pod-product-compliance
Lightning Source LLC
Chambersburg PA
CBHW022103170526
45157CB00004B/1458